Abba's Whisper

Abba's Whisper

Listening for the Voice of God

ALAN DAVEY AND ELIZABETH DAVEY
Foreword by Brian C. Stiller

WIPF & STOCK · Eugene, Oregon

ABBA'S WHISPER
Listening for the Voice of God

Copyright © 2017 Alan Davey and Elizabeth Davey. All rights reserved. Except for brief quotations in critical publications or reviews, no part of this book may be reproduced in any manner without prior written permission from the publisher. Write: Permissions, Wipf and Stock Publishers, 199 W. 8th Ave., Suite 3, Eugene, OR 97401.

Wipf & Stock
An Imprint of Wipf and Stock Publishers
199 W. 8th Ave., Suite 3
Eugene, OR 97401

www.wipfandstock.com

PAPERBACK ISBN: 978-1-4982-3684-3
HARDCOVER ISBN: 978-1-4982-3686-7
EBOOK ISBN: 978-1-4982-3685-0

Manufactured in the U.S.A.   JANUARY 10, 2017

"Window Conversation" excerpted from *Momentary Dark* by Margaret Avison, copyright © 2006. Reprinted by permission of McClelland & Stewart, a division of Penguin Random House Canada Limited.

"The Word" excerpted from *Always Now: The Collected Poems*, vol. 2, by Margaret Avison, copyright © 2004. Published by The Porcupine's Quill. Used by permission.

Scripture quotations are from the New Revised Standard Version, copyright © 1989, Division of Christian Education of the National Council of the Churches of Christ in the U.S.A. Used by permission. All rights reserved.

Contents

Foreword by Brian C. Stiller | vii

List of Drawings | ix

Abbreviations | xi

Introduction: Whisper in My Heart | xiii

Part I: The Paths of Listening | 1

   1 Praise: Living Above the Human Overcast | 3

   2 Creation: Small "S" Sacraments | 14

   3 Silence and Solitude: Into the Quiet | 24

   4 The Word: Manna from Heaven | 34

   5 Prayer: The Wings of Presence | 46

   6 The Community of Faith: Our Life Together | 58

   7 Celebration: The Song of the Heart | 69

Part II: The Practice of Listening | 79

   8 An Invitation to Pay Attention | 81

   9 A Journey in Time | 93

10 Service and Sacrifice as the Downward Way | 105

11 Light within the Struggle of Diminishment | 116

12 Creating Space | 128

13 Snail-Pace Discipleship | 140

14 The Cry of Absence | 152

Afterword | 165

Bibliography | 171

Foreword

"What was that you said?" The voice usually strong and resonant was a bare whisper. I dipped my ear closer to hear. His words I won't soon forget. If they had been in a normal tone, they would have lost their distinctive moment, mixed with surrounding chatter. When I speak, my voice is usually forceful; if reduced to a whisper, people strain forward to catch what they assume is the heart of the matter—what often they best remember.

An infant hears its mother's whispers. While the baby does not understand anything said, everything nevertheless is clear. The comfort of the whisper, be it a coo or "I love you," when felt, is intuitively deciphered. "Abba" is like a child's first word, a babbling of "Papa." It brings us to a childlike hearing—hearing not just what is being said, but what is intended. Walter Wangerin Jr. suggests that YHWH, the Hebrew word for the personal name of God, is a like a murmur, a breathing out, whispering carefully the name of the Most High. Without vowels, the consonants require one to press out air to make the sound, as he points out—a perfect symbol for our God, who is the source of the air we breathe, the life we live.

Twice a year, for some years now, seven of us involved in various public Christian ministries have spent a few days in learning to listen. Our guide takes us into various biblical texts then sends us away to listen. It has taken me some time to learn not to construct sermons, decipher texts, or propose fresh insights. All of us in our vocations are speakers, which means we are inclined to reflect on a text and then speak, as that is the most developed skill in our craft. One retreat, while reading a Gospel text, when asked what I heard during my hours of listening, I had one response: "I listened to John and watched Jesus."

The Daveys—Elizabeth and Alan—hear what I miss. Abba's Whisper is more than metaphorical. It is a guide to help me hear the gentle and quiet words set within the melodic lilt of eternity. The cognitive, logically examining of what is said roots us in texts to engage the mind, pressing us to agree, disagree, or rearrange. We hear speeches and listen to debate. But eternity is more. It is the collective wisdom of life, spoken in ways, times, and means that seeks to touch our whole being—Abba's whispering.

Let me suggest ways in which this richly textured, open and honest, and practical book may be used. First, as a personal guide, allow the seven chapters under Part I: The Paths of Listening to be read one chapter at a time, allowing a day to go by, absorbing its counsel, opening your inner life, and disciplining your active mind to learn the way forward as we learn to listen. Then move on to Part II: The Practice of Listening and test yourself on each chapter, as with Part I, giving yourself time to catch up to the idea, putting into practice what has surfaced in your reading.

Second, this book is perfectly suited to group study. It provides a fourteen-week guide, allowing for time between chapters if your group feels it needs more space to understand and test what is being learned. You will do your group a great service by introducing them to a fresh and biblical way of thinking about and experiencing our walk with God. It is a way of life—how we view time, how we bind ourselves to a community, how we pay attention in the moment, how we experience our own environment, how we deal with the aging process, and finally, how we receive life's inevitable diminishments with grace and hope.

Now free your heart and float downstream, learning to listen to the words of our Father, the whispering words of our loving Abba.

Brian C. Stiller
Global Ambassador
World Evangelical Alliance

List of Drawings

Yung Gul Kim, an architect and artist, left North Korea in 1947 and emigrated from South Korea after the Korean War in 1956. He studied art at UC Berkeley and earned his architecture degree from the University of Oregon. He makes his home in Seattle, Washington. Many of his drawings are from frequent hiking trips in the Northwest.

Part I "Smith Rock State Park, Oregon, '64"

Chapter 1 "Oregon Coast, Summer '64"

Chapter 2 "Summer '66"

Chapter 3 "Pause, Rest, Worship"

Chapter 4 "Pastoral Scene near Eugene, Oregon '62"

Chapter 5 "Tree Study 2"

Chapter 6 "Lumber Mill Pond on Siuslaw River near Florence, Oregon"

Chapter 7 untitled

Part II "Upstream McKenzie River, Summer '64"

Chapter 8 "By the Odell Creek at Willamette Pass '63"

Chapter 9 "Siuslaw River, Oregon, '65"

Chapter 10 "East of Sierra Mountains, California, Fall '94"

Chapter 11 untitled

Chapter 12 "Big Bear Lake '98"

Chapter 13 "Close to Crater Lake within Cascade Mountains '63"

Chapter 14 untitled

Afterword "Jeju Island, Korea"

Abbreviations

BAG   Bauer, W., W. F. Arndt, and F. W. Gingrich. *Greek-English Lexicon of the New Testament and Other Early Christian Literature*. Chicago: Universtity of Chicago Press, 1957.

NIDNTT   *The New International Dictionary of New Testament Theology*. Edited by Colin Brown. 3 vols. Grand Rapids: Zondervan, 1978.

OED   *Oxford English Dictionary*. Oxford: Oxford University Press, 2008.

TWOT   *Theological Wordbook of the Old Testament*. Edited by R. Laird Harris and G. L. Archer Jr. 2 vols. Chicago: Moody Press, 1980.

Introduction
Whisper in My Heart

IN C. S. LEWIS's children's story *The Magician's Nephew*, there is a moving scene of the great lion Aslan beginning his acts of creation, singing the new world of Narnia into existence. A cluster of disparate figures are present in the empty world watching the connection between light, hills, trees, animals emerging, and sounds coming from the lion's voice. The London cabbie and the children Jill and Digory are spellbound, silently drinking in the magnificent event. Jadis, the witch from the dying world of Charn, and Uncle Andrew, the magician who had deceived the children for his own purposes, are not charmed, and in fact are distracted, irritated, and chattering about their own agendas. The cabbie impatiently tells them to hush. "Watchin' and listenin's the thing at present."[1] Later in the story the children want Aslan to help Uncle Andrew out of his desperate predicament. Aslan's response is telling: "He has made himself unable to hear my voice."[2] There is a limit to what he can do for someone who is disconnected from spiritual desire.

"Listening's the thing right now," we agree, but listening is an art that we have not necessarily cultivated. In our ordinary lives we are often poor listeners. Students can be looking right at the teacher, seemingly attentive, but only half listening, and miss the instructions for an assignment. A friend gives directions to an out-of-the-way place; we start out well, but soon feel a loss of focus and end up hopelessly lost. When the doctor has some news of our medical condition we panic and miss crucial pieces of the diagnosis. When we are at an impasse in a conversation we do not hear the other person's position because we are planning our own retort. We

1. Lewis, *Magician's Nephew*, 125.
2. Ibid., 202–3.

Introduction

have difficulty maintaining attention during a lecture, sermon, or discussion. Even an intimate conversation between two friends can be derailed in failure to hear each other.

When we turn to matters of the heart, our ears may be stopped in inattentiveness and carelessness, fears and anxieties, preoccupations and stubborn desires. The spiritual life mirrors our outer life of distraction and we need help to hear the words of God. It is no wonder that Jesus spoke in parables and exclaimed, "Listen! . . . Let anyone with ears to hear listen!" (Mark 4:3, 9). He tells the story of the sower who goes out to sow seed, which falls on the unproductive soil of the path, rocky ground, and among thorns. Hope comes from a fourth place—falling into good soil and bringing forth grain (4:8); this success provides a paradigm for aspiring disciples. His interpretation for the parable is only given to those who stay with him "when he [is] alone" (4:10)—those prepared to really listen.

The traditional Chinese character embodying the idea of "listening" captures the intensity and intentionality that is needed to truly hear. It in-

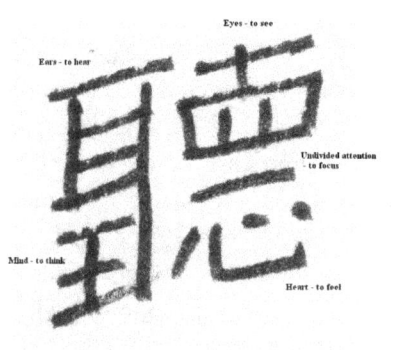

cludes five different symbols depicting "ears," "mind," "eyes," "undivided attention," and "heart." In some renditions these symbols are given a kind of story line: The "ear" is what one uses to listen; the "king" suggests one needs to pay attention as if the other person were king; "ten and eye" calls one to be observant as if one had ten eyes; "one" implies listening with individual attention; and "heart" points out that one listens with one's heart in addition to ear and eye. This complex of ideas illustrates that true listening is not a casual recognition of someone speaking but a real desire to hear and understand the intentions of the person. There is an assumption that the listener will respond in a meaningful way.

Jesus' figure of speech is the language of soil: there is the hard, unreceptive ground of the pathway. These are hearers of Jesus' words who, like Lewis's Uncle Andrew, are unable or unwilling to hear. The rocky ground implies possibility, but the words of Christ will not go deep into the hearer's hearts. The cluttered soil where the seed is choked by thorns signals listeners who are too distracted by life's cares to absorb the life-giving words. The disciple who is tuned in to listen to Jesus' words with heart, mind, and will

Introduction

to obey is the one spoken of as good soil. The cabbie and Digory and Jill, enrapt and excited by Aslan's creation, model this kind of discipleship as they go on to participate in Aslan's plans for Narnia.

There is a longstanding tradition that God whispers in our ears; he does not shout. It is in "the holy whisper," writes the Quaker mystic, that we hear Abba's voice, not in the noise of the clamoring crowds or the incessant barrage of social media.[3] From our deep Christian past we hear the voice of Augustine murmur, "*Whisper in my heart, I am here to save you*. Speak so that I may hear your words. My heart has ears ready to listen to you, Lord. Open them wide and *whisper in my heart, I am here to save you*. I shall hear your voice and make haste to clasp you to myself."[4] Augustine's prayer, in turn, points to two pivotal and familiar biblical stories that speak to the reality of Abba's whisper.

The first memorable story of hearing Abba's voice comes from the childhood of an early prophet during the tutelage of Samuel by Eli, the priest at Shiloh (1 Sam 3). The story begins with the boy Samuel sleeping in the temple and hearing a voice call out his name, "Samuel! Samuel!" Thinking it is the voice of Eli, he answers, "Here I am," and runs to him to see what he needs. Eli responds by curtly telling him to go back to bed because he did not call him. The same scenario happens twice more and on each occasion Samuel runs to Eli to provide assistance. Finally, Eli perceives that God is speaking to Samuel and he instructs him to respond to God's call with the answer, "Speak, Lord, for your servant is listening" (v. 9). Indeed, God not only speaks, but he comes down and stands before the boy uttering the double evocative "Samuel! Samuel!" The boy faithfully responds, "Speak, for your servant is listening" (v. 10). The narrative reminds us of God's quiet voice initially stirring the boy to wake up and pay attention to his call. It is so subtle that Eli hears nothing, and it has to happen three times before the aged priest provides guidance. On the other hand, Samuel is able to hear the gentle invitation of Abba and is receptive to Eli's instruction so that he might "know the Lord, and the word of the Lord" (v. 7) and enter into a faithful, listening relationship with God so that "none of his words [fall] to the ground" (v. 19).

The second narrative is found within the confines of Elijah's flight from the horrors of King Ahab and Queen Jezebel (1 Kgs 18–19). The context of the narrative reveals that through the power of God Elijah has

---

3. Kelly, *Testament of Devotion*, 93.
4. Augustine, *Confessions*, 24.

Introduction

defeated the prophets of Baal on Mount Carmel, demonstrated in fire from heaven completely consuming the sacrifices of the false prophets. Following the victory Elijah hears from Queen Jezebel that she desires to kill him, so he flees to Beersheba in the southernmost part of the Sinai Peninsula. Following a brief respite he continues his journey for forty days and reaches Mount Horeb, entering "the cave" (perhaps the very cave where Moses hid in the cleft of the rock; Exod 33:21–23) to hide from the evil queen and to ponder his gloomy situation. During this time of introspection Elijah is nudged by God to leave the confines of the cave, for the Lord is going to pass by and communicate with him even as he had for Moses. Responding to this premonition, the prophet goes outside and experiences a great storm raging with gale-like winds, ground-shaking earthquakes, and spontaneous fire outbreaks, but none of these make much impression on his frightened and saddened emotional overcast. Yet, following the pyrotechnics there is a "sound of sheer silence" and the narrative informs us that "when Elijah heard it, he wrapped his face in his mantle and went out and stood at the entrance of the cave" and hears the voice of God: "What are you doing here, Elijah?" (1 Kgs 19:12–13). It is not in the wind, the earthquake, or the fire but in the sound of sheer silence that Elijah senses the presence and hears the voice of God. In the silence God whispers the prophet's name and gains his attention to encourage and challenge him to re-engage his prophetic vocation.

Both stories speak of the need to pay attention and to listen for the interior small voice. God speaks quietly and invites the attentive and receptive heart to respond to his overtures of love. The passionate listening implied in the Chinese character above is what is needed and required to hear the subtle expressions of Abba's voice. It is like the gentle whisper of "sheer silence" in Elijah's ear or Samuel hearing his name whispered in the quiet of the night. God does not overwhelm us with his majestic presence; if he did we would automatically fall down in worship from awe or involuntary desire. Rather, God speaks quietly and respectfully so that we are not overpowered by his transcendence, but drawn by his love. Gerald May writes, "I think God refuses to be an object for attachment because God desires full love, not addiction. Love born of true freedom, love free from attachment, requires that we search for a deepening awareness of God, just as God freely reaches out to us."[5] God purposely remains elusive so that our finding of him is the fruit of an authentic passion to be whole and integrated into his

---

5. May, *Addiction and Grace*, 94.

Introduction

tapestry of abundant love. His love is never forced upon us. It is a gift that has to be received with both open hands and an open heart, demonstrated in an alertly listening ear.

It is demanding and stretching to listen—to even want to listen—in this manner. It is not surprising that we fill our space with background stimuli. There is the noise of television shows in our homes and the perpetual music in our ears as we drive and walk. We are unconsciously (or intentionally) obsessed with our cell phones, texting someone or simply surfing the continual stream of information on the Net. Frequently there is no specific purpose for these actions other than mere amusement, a desire to assuage boredom, or create a fleeting connection through a quick message. As a consequence, we need to do more than develop the art of listening. We must reach back to that desire, however hesitant, that the psalmist describes in dramatic terms: "My soul longs, indeed it faints, for the courts of the Lord" (Ps 84:2). We must, in a sense, wake up. "It is not easy to be sensitive to the delicate action of the Spirit," writes Catherine Doherty in *Poustinia*:

The Spirit moves so very lightly, lighter than the breeze, lighter than the air. When you breathe you are not aware of the air in the room. You are so used to breathing that you don't think about the air. The *poustinik* (i.e., "attentive hearer of God") must become conscious of the air.[6]

We need to train ourselves to listen for God's voice in this intentional manner. The path begins to present itself as we consider the ways that God speaks and the means he uses, drawing us to himself and communicating his unceasing love.

In the chapters that follow in the first part of this book we consider seven paths of listening. These may be familiar practices that we already consider important in our lives. Some we readily acknowledge but do not really engage in any intentional manner. Others seem less familiar avenues to open ourselves to Abba's whispers. The second part identifies seven challenges we may face in the practice of listening. Naturally, each of us has our unique proclivities and circumstances that may draw our attention to one or another of these situations. The questions at the end of each chapter help us determine specific attitudes or actions we may want to adopt.

At times we wonder, "Why does it matter if I hear from God? With the complications of my life I do not have time for additional metaphysical questions!" Certainly we live busy lives with many distractions—pressing family concerns, heavy workloads, financial headaches, and demanding

---

6. Doherty, *Poustinia*, 48.

Introduction

commutes! Whether or not we hear from God may not seem to be the most pressing issue as we draw up our daily agendas. Indeed, listening for his voice may be a helpful ideal, but practically an aspiration to pursue at a future point. We are called up short by Annie Dillard's blunt observation: "How we spend our days is, of course, how we spend our lives."[7] Our life story is comprised of our everyday living patterns. At some point our daily steps need to be embraced and slowed down so that the full sum of our days are held with meaning and purpose.

For this transformation of the spending of our days and lives to happen, we might consider the question of "living larger lives," a phrase coined by Henri Nouwen, which speaks to the reality of living full and abundant lives in the presence of God.[8] Living larger lives encompasses a perspective that embraces the everyday with a sense of vocation, purpose, and joy. It is derived from knowing life's source and allowing our lives to flow from it. It creatively spurs us on to make healthy, life-affirming choices. Largeness requires reclaiming the art of listening for Abba's voice amidst the cacophony of voices; otherwise, we get lost in the demands of the urgent moment. Largeness also invites us to take time to rest in the arms of the Beloved rather than rushing to utilitarian action. Finally, largeness nurtures patience and waiting for the *kairos* moment that leads us on the path towards effective and meaningful action. It is essential, not optional, to reclaim the art of listening, which provides a quiet counterpoint to the jarring sound bites of contemporary media. If we do not learn to listen, the sounds of the world will drown out the still, small, respectful voice of Abba and mask the fundamental purpose, in Kierkegaard's memorable words, of "willing one thing," which holds the deepest promise for our existence.

---

7. Dillard, *Writing Life*, 32.
8. Roderick, *Beloved*, 43–44.

PART I

The Paths of Listening

Chapter 1

Praise
Living Above the Human Overcast

WE BEGIN THIS JOURNEY to listen for Abba's whisper by choosing the path of praise. To live one's life anticipating hearing God's voice is to be mindful of his presence and activity in our world and to respond with gestures of gratitude and acknowledgement. In a lovely poem by the Canadian poet Margaret Avison, "Window Conversation: 'Brightness falls from the air,'" the speaker in the poem, looking out a window, sees the sun shine on the tip of a tree, and exclaims,

> The clouds, the morning
> sun are such that
> one lettuce-bright tree-tip
> over the roofs, like me,
> is singled out. We are
> sun-gilded.

This declaration "We are sun-gilded" exemplifies an attitude of praise. It is more than an acknowledgement of beauty; it is considering the source. For Avison, the sun is more than the sun; it is also a metaphor for God and his activity in creation. She imagines—or assigns what only humans can do—the tree's response: "You smile away / out there." And then, not to be

Part I—The Paths of Listening

outdone, she draws the landscape she is observing into her human response to these spots of pleasure:

> You are I am
> inexpert about timing.
> How this instant was
> hit upon is
> beyond us. We in
> passing can only receive
> this befalling, a
> blissed one.[1]

The poem comes from a heart and mind attuned to hearing God's voice and seeing God's work. The poet demonstrates a life pattern of awareness and gratitude, and offering her poem as gift to us, she passes on the possibility of our participation in the praise.

Our lives, of course, contain a mixture of "sun-gilded" moments and times of deep challenges and sometimes very loud trials of life. How do we hear the voice of God then? How do we hear the whisper of Abba when the darkness and difficulty seem to be all there is? In the film *Selma* there is a scene between Coretta and Martin Luther King Jr. where Coretta says, "I am living in the fog of death because of the constant threats to our family." Theirs was a particular point of crisis in the valiant effort expended on behalf of African Americans during the Civil Rights Movement of the 1960s. The same feeling can overtake any of us whether in ordinary or profound circumstances. We often feel that we are living in our own fog of death—or grief, pain, stress, anxiety, confusion, uncertainty, or chaos. Heavy indeed is the fog of life that encompasses us like a cloudbank covering the Avalon. How then do we overcome?

DECLARING YOUR PRAISES

When there is no obvious sun-gilded moment, the act of praise becomes an act of faith. We can still remain rooted in the voice of praise. Walter Brueggemann gives us a helpful point of reference when he admonishes us: "Remember 'who' you are by remembering 'whose' you are."[2] Abba's

---

1. Avison, "Window Conversation," *Momentary Dark*, 125–26.
2. Brueggemann, *Finally Comes the Poet*, 121.

hand is on the tiller and he will bring us through the stormy waters into safe harbor; and praise, the psalmists tell us, can be our access point to that harbor. Indeed, when we examine the Songs of Lament or Psalms of Disorientation, we note that though they begin in profound distress, they end with an exclamation of praise. Psalm 13 illustrates this movement beginning with a series of questions: "How long, O Lord? Will you forget me forever? How long will you hide your face from me? How long must I bear pain in my soul, and have sorrow in my heart all day long?" (vv. 1–2a). The psalmist follows this lamenting path until at the end he suddenly cries out: "But I trusted in your steadfast love; my heart shall rejoice in your salvation. I will sing to the Lord, because he has dealt bountifully with me" (vv. 5–6). We do not know when on his journey the psalmist came to this insight. Was it in the midst of his pain? Or did he reflect on his experience later with the wisdom of hindsight? What we do know is that the psalmist affirms that God remains faithful through it all and deserves praise even during challenging times.[3]

We are similarly invited to praise Abba through all of the seasons of our lives and in every type of weather. One way of doing this is to engage in what can be called declarative praise.[4] Anne Lamott expresses the formula in the most basic language: "Here are the two best prayers I know: 'Help me, help me, help me,' and 'Thank you, thank you, thank you.'"[5] When we thank God for what he has done we are engaging in declarative praise: "God, I thank you that the meeting I was anxious about went well." "Father, I thank you that you supplied a job for my son-in law." "Abba, thank you for restoring my friend to good health after his recent operation." These answered prayers deserve thanks and attention. God is hearing our concerns. God is with us. This is the spirit of declarative praise.

Declarative praise often has a public dimension as we tell others what God has done for us. We see this in the Psalms as the poets rise up within the assembly to utter their thanks: "Praise the Lord! I will give thanks to the Lord with my whole heart, in the company of the upright, in the congregation" (111:1). Or when Miriam leads the people in a song of thanks: "I will sing to the Lord, for he has triumphed gloriously; horse and rider he has thrown into the sea" (Exod 15:1). The writer of 1 Peter exclaims, "But you are a chosen race, a royal priesthood, a holy nation, God's own people that

---

3. See other psalms that follow this pattern of lament and praise, i.e., Pss 86, 35, 79.
4. See Westermann, *Praise and Lament in the Psalms*, 31–32.
5. Lamott, *Travelling Mercies*, 82.

you might declare the praises of him who called you out of darkness into his marvelous light" (2:9). When we tell others how God has acted on our behalf, we add our blessings to his great name through our word of witness.

Our two adult children were preparing to go on a vacation to the Bahamas with their small children and spouses. Right at that time, our granddaughter Violet came down with a fever. The doctor's opinion was that she would be fine to make the trip, but our anxiety remained. She was born with a heart defect called Tetralogy of Fallot, which required open-heart surgery when she was six months old. Though the operation was successful (and we praise God for that), there is a residue of concern for us around this little one. During their vacation Violet's fever worsened and the whole family became increasingly stressed. We started calling out to the faithful praying ones in our congregation, asking them to uphold Violet and intercede for her healing. The fever did not go away immediately but our children finished their vacation. Back in Canada the fever finally broke and Violet recovered. We have the option to say it was simply an illness from which Violet eventually recuperated—an unfortunate sickness during a long awaited holiday. But we can also choose the perspective of declarative praise, honoring God for healing Violet and rejoicing in his goodness with our community of faith! Abba heard the cries of his children and extended his healing hand. Our response is a choice—to praise God. Thank you, God, for your faithfulness in touching little Violet and restoring her to our family. Praise you, God, for being so good to us.

DESCRIBING (ADORING) GOD'S CHARACTER

A second form of praise is called descriptive praise, in which we worship God for his attributes.[6] Descriptive praise takes place in the Psalms of Orientation, where the psalmist enumerates the characteristics of God. These psalms have no hint of duress; there is just an enjoyment of the presence and activity of God. A good example is found in Psalm 8: "O Lord, our Sovereign, how majestic is your name in all the earth! You have set your glory above the heavens" (v. 1). The writer in Psalm 145 declares, "The might of your awesome deeds shall be proclaimed, and I will declare your greatness. They shall celebrate the fame of your abundant goodness, and shall sing aloud of your righteousness" (vv. 6–7). And in Psalm 33, we hear these words: "For the word of the Lord is upright, and all his work is done

---

6. Again, see Westermann, *Praise and Lament in the Psalms*, 31–32.

in faithfulness. He loves righteousness and justice; the earth is full of the steadfast love of the Lord" (vv. 4–5).[7] Descriptive praise reminds us of Abba's eternal qualities and of the truth that he is completely for us. The writer of Lamentations recapitulates this reality: "The steadfast love of the Lord never ceases, his mercies never come to an end; they are new every morning; great is your faithfulness" (3:22–23).

We add our descriptive praise by singing praises and adoring God for who he is: "I adore you for your amazing patience and love for me." "I lift you up as my strong tower, protector, and shepherd." "I praise you for your steadfast mercy, kindness, and compassion." We can carry these expressions of adoration and living prayer with us to help navigate the twists and turns of our day. In turn, we counteract the cultural mores that can so easily deflate us through the spirit of discouragement, hopelessness, and comparison. The responses of descriptive and declarative praise help to lift us above the human overcast. They act like a jet plane leaving the tarmac on an overcast day and carry us above the cloud bank to enter the sunshine and blue skies of the stratosphere. In turn, Abba raises us up above the storms of our lives to a place of rest and trust in his comforting presence. Yes, "we are sun-gilded" after all, however "inexpert we are about the timing!"

THE ROLE OF THANKSGIVING

Engaging in praise is moving toward thanksgiving and a life of gratitude. We recognize that our good God is bigger than life's problems and that the best thing that can happen to us has already happened in the person of Jesus. The authors of *Jubilate* express this attitude of gratitude as "wak[ing] up every morning and . . . know[ing] that no matter what the state of the world and of oneself, God is the loving God and so there is cause for joy."[8] Such an attitude opens up a myriad of opportunities as we focus on God's love. We are able to receive the blessings of the ordinary day with joy and thanks—regular things like home cooked food, an engaging conversation, a bright smile, a child's laugh, a warm touch. All of these gifts come alongside days that may be filled with problems, but the gifts remain good and are to be received with thanks. Edward Farrell reminds us of this curious mixture when he exclaims, "There are no perfect days, yet there are perfect moments in each day. Treasure them! Treasure your connectedness with

---

7. Other Psalms of Orientation include 19, 104, 133, and 131.
8. Hardy and Ford, *Jubilate*, 9.

nature, with the universe, history, others, the whole world."[9] We receive our lives from God and live in the reality of abundance, rejecting the worldly perspective of "not enough."

We need to be intentional every day in embracing the position that we have "more than enough." We can put expectations on ourselves—what Lewis Smedes calls "joy killers"—which create an unfortunate attitude of discontentment seeping into our hearts and minds. Lewis Smedes identifies three joy killers in his own life: the lust for virtue, total accountability, and problem catastrophizing—all experiences that place excessive demands on life and prevent the reception of joy.[10] We each have our own joy killers. I fall into a pattern of negative self-talk that denigrates my self-worth and dismisses my own value. I have to keep this negativity in check and replace these thoughts with life-enhancing affirmations. We all need to face our own demons, often ephemeral and undefined, and return to what is real and gives us joy. As we persist, gratitude has a way of dismantling even the most rigid systems built by complaint and negativity, replacing them with expressions of joy and creativity.

THE THERAPEUTIC ROLE OF PRAISE

A daily pattern of praise becomes a form of therapy. It is not simply a Pollyanna determination to live on the sunny side of life and refuse to accept the brokenness of the world. Praise is much more than that. It is deeply therapeutic because it has the power to penetrate the darkness, to enable the person who praises to see the One who is able to make all things well, who has the power and will to undo the injustice and pain of the world. Furthermore, praise draws us closer to God. When we praise God our communion is heightened and a greater sense of relationship is experienced. When we praise God there is a shift in focus from our own concerns to the glory of God. Through this change of perspective the peace of God is able to still our anxious hearts and fill us with confidence and assurance. Psalm 73 illustrates this shift from anxiety to peace. The psalmist is grieved by the injustice of life, where evil flourishes and righteous people suffer. As we read through the first seventeen verses we observe a descent into envy, confusion, and frustration, culminating in these words: "If I had said, 'I will talk on in this way,' I would have been untrue to the circle of your children. But

---

9. Farrell, *Beams of Prayer*, 146.
10. Smedes, *How Can It Be All Right?*, 26–31.

when I thought how to understand this, it seemed to me a wearisome task" (vv. 15–16). Thankfully, God provides the psalmist with insight as he enters into worship. He announces, "Until I entered the sanctuary of God; then I understood their final destiny" (vv. 16–17). The act of worship reveals his misinformed thoughts ("my soul was embittered") and he affirms, "But as for me, it is good to be near God; I have made the Lord God my refuge, to tell of all your works" (v. 28).

When we are aware of God's presence, his spirit is able to minister to us. The hurts, pains, and concerns of life take on a new perspective and cease to overwhelm. We can bear our sometimes heavy loads knowing that God is ultimately in control. And as our fears subside, we can move closer to God and experience his peace, care, and love. Praise also has the power to lift our despondency because the horizon is no longer filled with despair. When we praise we have the capacity to see a God who is greater than our sadness, and glimmers of light appear to dispel the darkness. I see an example of this uplifting power of praise in a Caribbean small group that is part of my faith community at Weston Park Baptist Church. The group meets each Thursday morning at seven in the room adjacent to my office. When I step foot into my office I am greeted by their wafts of praise and song and shouts of "Alleluia!" I know that these folk have their own deep concerns for family members, employment issues, and physical pain. But in their Thursday morning meetings they choose to revel in authentic praise that transcends their concerns. These Thursday mornings are an encouragement to my own state of mind and spirit—a reminder that Abba is there for us at any time if we will lift up our hearts to him. The psalmist says that the Lord "inhabits the praises of his people" (Ps 22:3 KJV), and nowhere do I see it more clearly than on Thursday mornings!

Praise also creates in us a sense of wholeness and even healing. We are created to be in relationship with God—to be in love with him. Praise is the most direct expression of this dynamic of love. When we praise him we have a sense of wholeness and rest and we move into that sphere of existence for which we were created. The humdrum of the world's affairs fades in significance to the experience of being alive in God. Within us there is an intuitive longing for God. When we praise him the longing begins to be satisfied and we find ourselves exclaiming, "Yes, this is what I am supposed to do. He is the one I am to know." The act of praise creates an attitude of gratitude for the gifts we receive from God. This sense of gratitude pervades our spirit and helps to combat the competitiveness and anxiety we often carry. The result is an inner peace that transforms the banal and low-grade depressions into a joy that Isaiah describes as "a crown of beauty instead of ashes, the oil of gladness instead of mourning, and a garment of praise instead of despair" (Isa 61:3). Praising God becomes a channel by which grace can stream into our lives and renew our sense of purpose and meaning. We are led along a path of wholeness that builds within us a reservoir of gratitude, thanksgiving, and love, enabling us to reach out to others with compassion.

Praise strengthens us in the role of service and care for others as we become re-energized in the task of walking with others and drawing on God's power. William Willimon writes of the necessity of praise—the intentional refocusing of our thoughts and energies towards the One who provides our emotional sustenance: "We withdraw in order to return," he explains, by which he is suggesting this deliberate act of praise and worship. "Without the withdrawal, we probably could not, would not return. For soon enough, the pain of the world grinds down and wears out the weak ones, the tired ones, the wounded ones. The wounds would bleed us to death were it not for the healing interlude of worship."[11] Worshipping God restores our strength and commitment to reach out to those who are hurting by regaining confidence in Abba's power to meet our collective needs.

The psalmists point to this restorative work of God proclaiming, "Blessed be the Lord, who daily bears us up; God is our salvation" (Ps 68:19) and "The Lord is faithful in all his words, and gracious in all his deeds. The Lord upholds all who are falling, and raises up all who are bowed down" (Ps 145:13b–14). Abba's commitment to empower and renew sustains us for the long journey of service and the challenge of faithful perseverance. My own Pentecostal upbringing, where praising God was central in our communal gatherings, and my experience of leading worship in churches, camps, and evangelistic meetings from my youth have deepened my passion for the praise of Abba. Praise for me has been a consistent source of spiritual sustenance.

PRAISING ENABLES US TO HEAR GOD'S VOICE

Praise allows us to see God's movements and hear God's voice in our daily routines by creating an environment of expectation and anticipation in the surprising works of Deity. We are connected to creation in a way that reveals the phenomenon of Abba's endearing presence in all that he has

---

11. Willimon, *Bible*, 95.

made. Brother David Steindl-Rast reminds us of how the epiphany of a rainbow or the flash of a red cardinal cries out to the nearness of God when he writes, "When that red streak shoots down on the rock like lightening on Elijah's altar, I know what e.e. cummings means, 'The eyes of my eyes are opened.'"[12] Similarly, the V-formation of Canada geese flying over the concrete towers of Toronto towards the shores of Lake Ontario strikes me us a serendipitous expression of God's amazing presence. Or the explosion of life that late spring brings to a Great Lakes city with the sudden arrival of robins, blue jays, and cardinals, and the blanket of verdancy that unfolds over the city in a matter of days. Driving on an onramp to the 427 Freeway the other day, I almost collided with an outstretched golden-winged hawk sweeping down for prey within feet of my driver's window—a God-moment worthy of praise as the urban and natural world were woven together.

When we praise God, the subliminal, eternal connections of our DNA bubble up to the surface. A spirit of gratefulness and our articulated yes to God crystallizes what is so often hidden. It is essential that we pay attention to these little sun-gilded moments. Such occasions hold the possibility of doors opening in a moment that we have been waiting for years to occur. It is like the children of Narnia opening a wardrobe door to find themselves in a stunning new world. It is hiking through an Andean desert and coming across a flowering cactus—an event that happens once every hundred years. So we are offered new worlds daily if we have the eyes to see and, more importantly, the receptive ears to hear so that we open the doors and explore what is being given.

The dilemma we face in our day-to-day living is to keep saying yes even as the fog of life sometimes envelops us. In these times we need to praise Abba more than ever. We return to the film *Selma*, where Martin Luther King Jr. is considering his plans to march from Selma to Birmingham. He is distraught because he knows the safety of his fellow marchers is at risk if he follows through with the unsanctioned protest. In desperation he makes a late-night phone call to his friend Mahalia Jackson. He mumbles to his friend, "I need to hear the voice of the Lord." She sits up in bed, saying, "All right, Martin" and starts singing into the phone,

---

12. Steindl-Rast, *Gratefulness*, 9–11.

Part I—The Paths of Listening

> Precious Lord, take my hand, lead me on, help me stand,
> I am tired, I am weak, I am worn;
> Thro' the storm, thro' the night, Lead me on to the light.
> Take my hand, precious Lord, lead me home.[13]

Through these words of praise lifted up by the singer, King receives the consolation to press on. Praise matters! Praise is effective! Praise dispels the human overcast that so often obscures the presence of God and takes away our joy. In the words of Brother David, "The human heart is made for universal praise . . . Love wholeheartedly, be surprised, give thanks and praise—then you will discover the fullness of your life."[14] Let us, along with the Scriptures, "Declare the praises of him who called you out of darkness into his marvelous light" (1 Pet 2:9). Let us declare the praises! Count our blessings! See God's goodness! Let us be attentive to the quiet rustling of the Spirit—the whisper of Abba—and respond with thanks and gratitude to the Giver of Life.

---

13. Dorsey, *Precious Lord, Take My Hand*.
14. Steindl-Rast, *Gratefulness*, 3–4.

PRAISE

QUESTIONS FOR REFLECTION

1. Write down three statements of declarative praise that indicate your awareness of God's blessings in your life.
2. Meditate upon three aspects of descriptive praise that energize your relationship with Abba.
3. Consider how praise is a therapeutic spiritual discipline in your faith journey. List the ways that engaging in the praise of God brings you healing.
4. What is the greatest challenge you face for remaining in an attitude of praise?
5. Write down areas in your life where a spirit of praise might initiate healing in your relationships with others.

Chapter 2

Creation
Small "S" Sacraments

FOGO ISLAND

The ocean is one of my passions. Mesmerized by the vastness of blue, I love to lose myself in the sound of breaking waves. So when a friend invited me to spend ten days hiking the Newfoundland east coast trails with an ocean vista as our guide, I immediately said yes. We began our adventure in the sleepy fishing village of Twillingate. After several days of hiking the coast and eating fresh seafood cuisine, we travelled to Farewell and took the ferry to Fogo Island, the largest island off the east coast of the province. Fogo is a mystical place: a barren windswept frontier covered by small brush and a myriad of berries, some tantalizingly sweet and others deadly. It also boasts Brimstone Head, one of the five corners of the Flat Earth Society of Canada from which one can peer toward the distant edge of the earth.

Another interesting feature of the island is the Fogo Island Inn, a five-star hotel built by Zita Cobb, an islander who made her fortune in the California high-tech world. The inn is part of the small community of Joe Batt's Arm, built perilously high over the crashing waters below and perfect for fall storm watchers! Zita Cobb has built a series of studios around the island that match the wilderness motifs, where artists are invited to apply their craft using these isolated stations as home and inspiration. This juxtaposition of wild landscape and human creativity rejoices in divine and human creativity, reminding me of the declaration from Irenaeus that "the glory of God is the human person fully alive."[1] Exploring the island, a sacramental quality emerged as I experienced Abba's presence in both his divine handiwork and in the creativity of his creatures.

SMALL "S" SACRAMENTS IN CREATION

The word "sacrament" has traditionally referred to a spiritually symbolic act or object, including such actions as Communion and baptism or other solemn ceremonies such as marriage and confirmation. In baptism, we go under the water or are sprinkled with water as we experience new life in Christ. Paul rejoices as he describes the false self washed away and the new self rising to life through the act of baptism (Rom 6:1–4). In Communion we eat the bread and drink the wine as physical actions that speak to us of sharing in our union with Jesus (1 Cor 11:23–25). These become sacramental actions as they speak to the spiritual truths they represent.

In a widened application, other objects or actions can take on sacramental significance as they become channels pointing us to God or vehicles by which we give ourselves to God. It is revealing that the *Oxford English Dictionary*'s explanation of "sacrament" cites R. Inge writing in *Christian Mysticism*, "To the true mystic, life itself is a sacrament." When we experience creation as a sign pointing us to God, or when we offer our daily experiences as a praise offering, we are participating in the sacramental life as a way of knowing Abba and hearing his whisper.[2] The broader meaning of "sacrament" declares that God is praised through all creation. Everything that he has created can be seen as a sign pointing to God, pointers which become small "s" sacraments, directing us to the creator of life. The authors of *Jubilate* write, "Creation's praise is not an extra, an addition to what it is, but is the shining of its being, the overflowing significance it has in pointing

---

1 Jean Vanier, *Drawn into the Mystery of Jesus*, 295.

2. The English word "sacrament" does not have a specific Hebrew or Greek counterpart. The word is derived from the Latin *sacrāmentum*, which is related to *sacrāre*—"to consecrate," "to set apart." The basic meaning of the word is taken from the root *săcer*—"holy," "dedicated," "set apart" (*OED*).

Part I—The Paths of Listening

to its Creator simply by being itself."³ These created things become reminders to us of God's presence, inviting us to give praise to the giver of life.

It is a common theme in Scripture that creation declares the handiwork of God. The Psalms speak of God's voice being heard in thunder and lightening (29: 3–7) and all of heaven, earth, and seas praising him (69:34; 97:6; 98:7–8). The prophet Isaiah announces the mountains, forests, and trees displaying the glory of God (Isa 44:23). The prophet Joel adds that the wild animals, open pastures, trees bearing fruit, and vines producing crops all speak of God's provision and presence (Joel 2:21–22). Ezra sums up the beneficence of God praising him for his goodness in giving the gift of life: "You are the Lord, you alone; you have made heaven, the heaven of heavens, with all their host, the earth and all that is in them. To all of them you give life, and the host of heaven worships you" (Neh 9:7). These are just a sample of the emphasis in the Scriptures on God's work in creation and their reflection of his glory and presence.

So what do we do with God's gift of creation? At times, we might be highly intentional in seeking to hear Abba's voice. I remember one such experience when I was in a monastic setting in the countryside meadows of Ontario for ten days of meditation, quiet, and spiritual renewal. I had completed this retreat on numerous occasions but never in the month of May. This time the surrounding nature was exalted. The forest floor was exuberantly covered in white trilliums, the trees creaked and groaned in the flowing winds, the birdlife was plentiful with new arrivals from abroad, including multiple sightings of Baltimore orioles, rarely seen in Toronto. The prayer sessions were announced with the ringing of a sonorous gong penetrating the far reaches of the forest, calling us to stillness and prayer. The total silence of the retreat spoke of intentionality and purpose—a desire to quiet inner and outer busyness. All of these tangible factors joined to provide a rich environment for reflection and listening for Abba's voice.

At the same time, his whisper is heard in the ordinary and everyday experience of the one who has the eyes and ears to discern his subtle ways. The same kind of experience can occur in the midst of activity not specific to spiritual meditation. Recently, I experienced God's creative presence while diving the waters of Grand Cayman. I had dove the sister islands of Little Cayman and Cayman Brac some ten years earlier, but never the largest of the three islands. I was initially disappointed at what I found in Grand Cayman: a tourist barrage, with its daily arrivals of cruise ships, each a floating

---

3. Hardy and Ford, *Jubilate*, 192.

city housing thousands of people. Every ship disturbs the fragile underwater marine system through pollution and noise as it shuttles traffic over the reefs. As we dove over the week we saw the regular Caribbean sea life, but overall the fishlife was less prolific than what I had experienced on the more isolated sister islands. I got a little desperate and found myself praying, "Lord, let me experience something unusual in your water world today!"

As it happened, while diving a series of shallow caves linked with a formation of narrow channels, we came upon a school of tarpon tucked under a coral shelf sheltered from the current. Tarpon are wild-looking sport fish sought after by fishermen who love challenging battles! Their skin is covered with shiny scales that flash in the sun and their body shape resembles the long-torsoed barracudas with their extended mouth and sharp teeth. They have no fear. Suspended motionless in the water, peering into my eyes, they dared me to approach. It was both unnerving and exciting to share their space, and upon reflection it was an amazing gift from God—something I had not seen since diving Key Largo fifteen years previously. Abba showed up for me that day, whispering in my ear, amidst thirty or forty tarpon! While resting under a coral shelf those tarpon glistened like stars and became a sacramental sign to a grateful Canadian diver.

SMALL "S" SACRAMENTS IN HUMAN CREATIVITY

The apostle Paul expands the sacramental dimension to include both creation and the creativity of humanity. In an insightful manner Paul reminds the Philippian church, "Finally, beloved, whatever is true, whatever is honorable, whatever is just, whatever is pure, whatever is pleasing, whatever is commendable, if there is any excellence and if there is anything worthy of praise, think about these things" (Phil 4:8). His statement draws on both the cardinal virtues from classical antiquity—wisdom, justice, temperance, and courage—and the familiar Christian virtues of faith, hope, and love. The apostle's list of whatever is true, honorable, just, pure, and commendable describes aspects of excellence and goodness that open up a vast world to our senses. Paul encourages his readers to focus on the healthy stuff of life that builds rather than tears down life. He encourages us to stir our imaginations, cast our hearts and minds upon goodness and fecundity, and then act on those life-enhancing movements. Tom Wright leads us in this direction, phrasing it in the negative, when he asks:

Part I—The Paths of Listening

> How are you going to celebrate the goodness of the creator if you feed your mind only on the places in the world which humans have made ugly? How are you going to take steps to fill your mind instead with all the things that God has given us to be legitimately pleased with, and to enjoy and celebrate?[4]

We are invited—indeed, exhorted—to consider those things which speak of truth, beauty, and goodness. This focus produces joy and abundance, lifting us toward celebrating the gift of life. A Mozart symphony, an Emily Carr painting, a Dostoyevsky novel, or a Rodin sculpture can inspire and encourage the awareness of Abba's whisper. A student's well-written essay, a child's piano recital, a baseball game played well, a homemade dinner—these more ordinary encounters with family and friends near and far can produce the same glorious effect. In fact, there are countless expressions and realities that become small "s" sacraments declaring the beautiful presence of God among us.

The poet Gerard Manley Hopkins affirms these opportunities in striking and peculiar observations in his famous poem "Pied Beauty":

> Glory be to God for dappled things—
> > For skies of couple-color as a brinded cow;
> > For rose-moles all in stripple upon trout that swim;
> Fresh-firecoal chestnut falls; finches' wings:
> > Landscape plotted and pieced—fold, fallow and plough;
> > And all trades, their gear and tackle and trim.
>
> All things counter, original, spare and strange;
> > Whatever is fickle, freckled (who knows how?)
> > With swift, slow; sweet, sour; adazzle, dim;
> He fathers-forth whose beauty is past change:
> > Praise Him.[5]

The poet calls attention to the beauty found in "dappled things"—having spots or patches of color, mottled and patterned things. His list is startlingly varied with skies, cows, trout, finches. Moving seamlessly from the divine handiwork to human activity, he notes the landscape that has been "plotted and pieced"—arranged in variety as people have subdued the earth through farming, trades, and all manner of development. In the closing lines of the

---

4. Wright, *Paul for Everyone: The Prison Letters*, 131–32.
5. In Abrams and Greenblatt, eds., *Norton Anthology of English Literature*, 2160.

poem, "He fathers-forth whose beauty is past change: / Praise Him," the poet suggests that the whisper of Abba may be heard by those who notice and celebrate.

Diving and music speak sacramentally to me in a powerful way. With diving there is not only the beauty of the underwater world, but the experience of navigating the gear, tackle, and trim essential to the sport. As I handle the tanks, adjust the regulator, play with the computer, regulate my buoyancy, and control the function of my drysuit, I find myself sacramentally preparing to enter the vast ocean environment. Every piece of equipment plays a vital role. Similarly, when it comes to music, my passion is not only for the varied sounds that inspire—from Mozart to Bartók, jazz to pop to gospel—but the instruments themselves. In my case—guitars!—I have developed a collection over the years: a blond maple Gibson L4, a cedar Taylor, an ash Telecaster, an acoustic from La Paz made from the South American dark rich woods of picana negra, jacaranda, and nogal. Each one feels different in my hands—the combination of wood type, body design, necks, and strings—and has its own sound and its own character. Each has done its own journey with me. Each one is a small "s" sacrament resonating Abba's presence and whisper through his creation and human design.

God uses an infinite variety of means in drawing his children to himself: wood, stone, paper, sky, wind, mountains, water, music, art, dance, stories, drama, film, oration, play, sports—the list is truly endless. The story is told of a seventeen-year-old Charles Spurgeon turning into a small Methodist chapel in London during a severe snowstorm. He happened upon a humble preacher delivering the words of Jesus, saying "Look to me." Spurgeon says he looked and his life was changed. He postulates that without the snowstorm he would not have turned into the chapel and may never have discovered the life-changing presence of Jesus. The snowstorm and the preacher's inviting words became sacramental events for Spurgeon.[6] Across the pond, the great scientist-philosopher Teilhard de Chardin, while walking in Central Park with his young friend Jean Huston, came across a "spectacular" caterpillar. He fell onto his knees and pressed his nose into the face of the little creature and encouraged Jean to do the same. He was so amazed that such a creature could both be beautiful and surprisingly appear in the center of a great metropolis that he began to sing its praises to Jean and passing pedestrians. A

---

6. Bush and Nettles, *Baptists and the Bible*, 243–45.

PART I—THE PATHS OF LISTENING

scientific appreciation, an adventurous caterpillar, and a cacophonous city milieu all joined together enabling God's beauty to shine through.[7]

In her little house on Tinker Creek, a modern-day prophet completely understands the sacramental dimension of life. Annie Dillard ends her delightful book *Pilgrim at Tinker Creek* with these words of joy:

> A sixteenth-century alchemist wrote of the philosopher's stone, "One finds it in the open country, in the village and in the town. It is in everything which God created. Maids throw it on the street. Children play with it." The giant water bug ate the world. And like Billy Bray I go my way, and my left foot says, "Glory," and my right foot says, "Amen": in and out of Shadow Creek, upstream and down, exultant, in a daze, dancing, to the twin silver trumpets of praise.[8]

Dillard's experience of God is that he shows up in our world constantly if we take the time to pause and actually look at what is happening around us. He dances in every corner of his creation if we only have eyes to see, and whispers to us if we have ears to hear.

SMALL "S" SACRAMENTS AS SYMBOLS

Besides creation and human creativity, small "s" sacraments can be types, signs, or symbols.[9] The Bible itself is full of symbols that stand for religious truths or realities.[10] "Candles" or "lamps" symbolize Jesus as the light of the world (Rev 21:23); the "cross" represents the sacrifice of Jesus (Col 2:14); a "throne" (Matt 19:28), "scepter" (Heb 1:8), "robe" (Rev 19:13), and "crown" (Rev 19:12) all symbolize the power and rule of Christ in the kingdom of

---

7 Huston, *Mystical Dogs*, 33. For the complete story see Jean Huston, Facebook, July 6, 2014.

8. Dillard, *Pilgrim at Tinker Creek*, 271.

9. The *OED* defines the word "symbol" as "something that stands for, represents, or denotes something else . . . especially a material object representing or taken to represent something immaterial or abstract."

10. The word "symbol" is derived from the Greek *symbolon*, which joins the two Greek words *syn* ("with") and *bole* ("to throw"), meaning literally "to put together'" (*OED*). The word *symbolon* is not used in the Greek New Testament but the concept is contained in the words *typos*, from which we derive "type"; *eidolon*, translated as "'image" or "idol"; and *eikōn*, as "image," "likeness," or "appearance." These words are exemplified in the following texts: Heb 8:5 refers to the Old Testament priestly model as a "type" of the heavenly realities; 1 Cor 10:28 speaks of the pagan gods as "idols" in contrast to the true God; and Rom 8:29 uses *eikōn* in reference to individuals regaining the image of God through the indwelling presence of the Holy Spirit.

CREATION

God. We engage symbols regularly in our daily living. As people of faith we may wear crosses around our necks linking us with the person of Jesus. In our churches we use stained glass to tell the stories of the Gospels; our Communion tables and pulpits with the Latin letters "INRI" stand for the roles Jesus encapsulates; or perhaps, as in Tyndale's University Chapel, the stories of the Stations of the Cross are carved ornately in marble.[11] Outside the church we might display fish bumper stickers, quietly telling others we are faithful followers (hopefully also expressed in safe and courteous driving!). We light Advent candles counting down the four weeks of Advent in our home, or light a candle before we contemplate the Scriptures and pray. In our own home we have a framed photograph of a plaque from the Abbey of Gethsemani (made famous by Thomas Merton) hanging inside our front door: "Let all guests that come be received like Christ." These words are sacramental, reminding us to be a light for Christ to whoever may enter.

If we understand how symbols function they can be key access points to God. In *Worship*, Evelyn Underhill explains, "For the symbol, or significant image, is not, as its unfriendly critics suppose, a substitute for spiritual truth. It is rather the point where physical and metaphysical meet—a half-way house, where the world of things and world of spirit unite, and produce a new thing."[12] The symbols become sacramental as they channel our attention toward some characteristic or aspect of God, linking us to him. Religious truths penetrate our hearts and minds through the use of symbols in a way that rational, objective propositions cannot. In *Worship Is a Verb*, Webber echoes Underhill's understanding that we have placed such an emphasis upon "verbal, logical and verifiable truth," that sign communication has almost been lost.[13] Symbols communicate on an intuitive level to the parts of us that do not learn through objective data, revealing spiritual realities directly to the heart. As a result, it is essential to regain the use of signs and symbols as channels for knowing and hearing God. The inclusion of the objective (scriptural truth) and subjective dimensions of truth (experience) reinforce each other and deepen the impact of our religious experience.

My own faith journey has been supported in this way. I have a stone cross from Sligo, Ireland, which helps me. Its weight, roughness, and beauty

---

11. The four letters INRI are the abbreviation for the Latin inscription meaning "Jesus of Nazareth, King of the Jews," placed by Pilate over the head of Jesus on the cross.

12. Underhill, *Worship*, 40.

13. Webber, *Worship Is a Verb*, 83.

Part I—The Paths of Listening

encompassed by a Celtic circle speak to me of the Trinity, who provides the hope of eternal life. Hanging in my church office is an image of the Christ Pantocrator from the Hagia Sophia (The Church of the Holy Wisdom) in Istanbul, which presents the wisdom and life-giving power of the resurrected Christ (often depicted filling the dome of Eastern Orthodox churches). In my home study, I use daily a meditation blanket and pillow that speak of prayer, trust, and confidence in Abba. These tangible objects help on a sensory level and support my faith journey, which, at times, can seem ethereal and distant.

When we come from traditions where the inclusion of symbols is not regularly practiced, we may feel uncomfortable. Choosing symbols that resonate with our own experience, particularly in private times with God, can prevent awkwardness and self-consciousness within our faith communities. Using them in meditation and prayer can open up new connecting points with Abba. The use of a lit candle during prayer or a figure of a shepherd caring for his sheep or a bell rung to initiate listening for his voice can be powerful symbols to create focus. Sometimes listening to music during prayer can be an avenue for calm and experiencing God's presence. Paul echoes similar sentiments when he encourages us "to speak to one another and to God through psalms, hymns and spiritual songs" (Eph 5:19–20; Col 3:16). Music has a sacramental capacity enabling us to connect with the *mysterium tremendum*, as evidenced through a global practice of worship through musical form.

How do we listen for Abba's voice? God speaks through each moment of our everyday existence. His voice in creation affirms his presence in stunning beauty and in surprising ways. As a result, we are invited to pay attention to Abba's subtle murmurs that appear through his graced hand in creation. Human creativity also reveals Abba's touch through a myriad of expressions of joy, excellence, and the full palate of human emotion. Be it music or art, science or mathematics, philosophy or astronomy, why not give ourselves to the voices that lead to integration and spiritual wholeness? As the Scriptures encourage, let us fill our minds with the good things that build and promote personal growth and development. Finally, the design and employment of symbols within the rhythm of our lives reveals God's grace and activity. Once again a world of possibilities exist for our consideration. A symbol only gains power as it is chosen and filled with meaning that opens up spiritual truth for one's personal journey. Together these three avenues communicate God's enlivening presence in the day to day. As

CREATION

we open our eyes and tune our senses to hear God's voice his whispers waft throughout our experiences and we know his sacramental touch.

QUESTIONS FOR REFLECTION

1. What aspects of creation impress you with God's touch and presence? Why do these dimensions speak powerfully in your experience?

2. Are there creative expressions that assist you in connecting with God? In what way are these forms helpful in your spiritual pilgrimage?

3. Evelyn Underhill reminds us that "symbols become meeting points between the physical and metaphysical world." What significant images (or symbols) are beneficial for you and why?

4. Share your spiritual connecting points with a friend and have them share theirs with you. Be aware of the amazing variety that speaks to our spiritual journeys.

Chapter 3

Silence and Solitude: Into the Quiet

San Salvador is a small island in the outer Bahamas known for two diverse facts. First, it was Christopher Columbus's original landing point as he sought out the new world. A simple cross serving as a monument for this civilization-changing event stands on one of its beaches. Second, it is an island known—at least among divers—for the abundance of hammerhead sharks that cruise the island's walls.

My friend and I travelled to the island for the sharks. We arrived via a small plane from Nassau and were greeted by wild surf and a strong on-shore wind, an unusual combination for the island, which normally boasts calm seas and clear water. As we chatted with other divers, it became clear that we were indeed in for some challenging diving conditions. The fortunate turn in the trip for me was how the pounding surf turned into something sacred. Each morning I found myself rising earlier and earlier at my isolated lodge to walk the deserted beach. What began as disappointment with the diving prospects ended with healing times as I basked in the surf, sandpipers, and wind clattering the nearby palm trees. And as we persisted with the diving in spite of the wind and waves and poor visibility, I even came face to face with a curious hammerhead as we cruised the outer walls. In fact, I almost bumped straight into his startled head. It was a surreal moment as we peered into each other's eyes before he slowly turned and disappeared into the abyss.

SILENCE AND SOLITUDE: INTO THE QUIET

The absence of human clamor and the symphony of nature's chorus were profoundly impactful during those days on San Salvador. The week of endless waves cleansed my spirit and reminded me of our inner oceans that await exploration as we acknowledge their beckoning. I am reminded of Thomas Kelly's words drawing us into such depths:

> For over the margins of life comes a whisper, a faint call, a premonition of richer living which we know we are passing by . . . we have hints that there is a way of life vastly richer and deeper than all this hurried existence, a life of unhurried serenity and peace and power. If only we could find the Silence which is the source of sound.[1]

It is this realm of quiet that invites exploration as we reflect on the poet's thoughts in Psalm 62.

WAITING IN SILENCE

Psalm 62 begins with the declaration, "For God alone my soul waits in silence; from him comes my salvation. He alone is my rock and my salvation, my fortress; I shall never be shaken" (vv. 1–2). The word translated as "silence" is the Hebrew word *dûmâ*, which has the sense of "being motionless, to keep silence, to last."[2] Waiting in silence in the psalmist's sense is like gazing on the beauty of Lake Louise on a windless afternoon without a ripple to be seen on its aqua blue surface. The psalmist sits with this silence and declares that his trust is in God alone even amidst the challenges of his life.[3] He acknowledges that he is under attack from his enemies: "How long will you assail a person, will you batter your victim, all of you, as you would a leaning wall, a tottering fence?" (v. 3). Sitting on a perilous wall, he is confident God will protect him from falling as he declares to the surrounding community that "[God] alone is his rock, and his salvation, his fortress; he shall never be shaken" (v. 2).[4] Indeed, he feels secure in God's hand despite the daunting challenges facing him. Once again he repeats the call for silence: "For God alone my soul waits in silence, for my hope is from him" (v. 5). This declaration takes the form of self-talk as he reminds

---

1. Kelly, *Testament of Devotion*, 92.
2. *TWOT*, 186.
3. It is important to note that the word "alone" is used six times in these early verses of the psalm (vv. 1, 2, 4, 5, 6, 9), emphasizing its importance to the writer's thinking.
4. See Knight, *Psalms*, 285.

himself that God is his deliverance and refuge (vv. 6–7). He knows that God is there but he also knows that amidst such opposition there is power in rehearsing his outlook and trust in God. The psalmist ends the unit by again announcing to all who hear that God is his rock, salvation, fortress, honor, refuge, and deliverance. These declarations become names for God.

"Fortress" or "tower" speaks of the security one experiences in God. As the wisdom writer states, "The name of the Lord is a strong tower; the righteous run to it and are safe'" (Prov 18:10 NIV). This image reminds me of a twelfth-century round tower I walked around in Kildare, Ireland, at St. Brigid's Cathedral, which served to protect the people from enemies' assaults. Individuals would enter the stone tower, prepared with provisions, and wait out the sieges protected by the fireproof walls. In a similar way God is our "round tower" who protects and sustains us amidst the vicissitudes—the attacks and sieges—of life. We find our strength in our relationship with him as his word provides confidence and trust amidst the shifting sands of the values of popular culture. It reminds us of the importance of healthy self-reflection as we journey. Do we yell at ourselves and use language that belittles our self worth? Or do we remind ourselves that Abba journeys with us and supports us no matter what we come up against?

The psalmist ends his reflection with a comparison of what could be called "shadow and substance."[5] The things of shadow include wealth and power (ironically, values that our world applauds), which the psalmist says "are altogether lighter than a breath" (v. 9), or as one commentator translates, "On scales they are lighter than leaves, together lighter than vapor."[6] The psalmist boldly exhorts the community not to be deceived by the world's focus on fame, money, or possessions for they have no lasting value; and in the balance of life such accretions are lighter than air. Rather, he encourages the faithful to trust in the substance and permanence of the power and steadfast love of God (v.v 11–12). In contrast to wealth often gained by inheritance or simply good fortune, God's power is not limited. God as creator is all-powerful and his domain includes the entire earth, and the prophet's use of "God's outstretched hand" and "God's right hand" emphasizes this awesome strength (Jer 21:5; 27:5). God is also all-loving, as the Hebrew word *ḥesed* ("steadfast love") suggests, and he extends his love liberally to all those who live with open hands, ready to receive his good

---

5. Kidner, *Psalms 1–72*, 222.
6. Dahood, *Psalms 51–100*, 90.

gifts. God's love contrasts greatly with love the world can offer—limited, finite, sometimes fickle, oftentimes self-serving.

Intellectually, we know the truth of these contrasts; we believe God's power and love are greater than material prosperity. But daily, sellers and managers of wealth seduce us externally, and our own insecurity and anxiety sway us internally. We push enormous weights in front of us, as the great fourteenth-century poet Dante points out, as we lead undiscerning and undistinguished lives.[7] When the psalmist exclaims, "If riches increase, do not set our heart on them" (v. 10), we do not quite believe him in our hearts or practically live out that freedom. To alter this destructive focus we need to replace the voices in our heads with the quieter whisper of Abba, bringing us back full circle to the opening of Psalm 62: "For God alone my soul waits in silence" (v. 1).

EMBRACING SILENCE AND SOLITUDE

The practice of silence is a difficult discipline to embrace. We are used to busyness as the normal practice of life. We run from activity to appointment to coffee date to class, as we jam-pack our days. Filling our agendas relates to the mores of our culture as we live in a society that rewards activity and accomplishment. We feel important and valued when we are busily engaged, so we stay on the run, seeking out competition and grasping ways to gain advantage over others. Our freneticism also speaks of our desire for control. If we are busy and manage our lives, we can orchestrate the desired results. Furthermore, we have been taught to seek out solutions and to be active in working out our problems. We have been trained to be busy and to get things done. More work, money, knowledge, and power are the answers to our problems.

The idea of waiting in silence is interesting at a theoretical level, but in actuality our inclination is usually to act and make something happen. This incessant activity is heightened by the reality that we live and act at what Dallas Willard calls the "epidermal" level of self, the point of first contact (which is the level of sensation).[8] We react automatically. If something feels good, we like it and go toward it. If something is unpleasant, we experience the opposite and recoil from the sensation. As we live our lives on the sur-

---

7. See Canto 7 of Dante's *Inferno*, where the "prodigal" and the "miserly" sinners in the fourth circle of hell live out their obsession.

8. Willard, *Divine Conspiracy*, 358.

face level, we keep responding to stimuli, some of which we find pleasant and desire, and others unpleasant and wish to end. This superficial response keeps us in a cycle of reaction, promoting anxiety, restlessness, and angst. We constantly seek pleasure over pain and have revulsion to sensations that bring discomfort. For example, I love coffee. I love the taste, smell, and slow process of drinking a cup of finely brewed coffee. Yes. But on a deeper level, I enjoy the stimulating effect coffee has on my body. I seek the kick that coffee offers! My enjoyment of coffee is directly related to the energizing sensation it provides and not simply to its taste. On the other hand, I hate brussels sprouts! I have a physical reaction to this benign vegetable due to early memories of being forced to eat it. The physical sensation it induces is one of revulsion. My family, even including my young granddaughter, loves them and cannot understand my forceful reaction. The problem is not the actual vegetable but the negative sensation that is associated with it. Consequently, as we live our lives at this epidermal level, we are caught up in a cycle of desire and aversion, posing significant challenges for navigation on a daily basis.

The way out of this dilemma is to train ourselves not to remain in positions of reaction. We do this through the twin disciplines of *silence* and *solitude*.[9] Silence and solitude lead us into a different way of living—a more tranquil way—into a space of trust and faith, where we can let go of our incessant activity and trust that God will open up the ways that are best for us. It is the difference of living with clenched fists or with open hands.[10] Clenched fists articulate, "I must do it all!" Open hands allow for relaxation and synergy. We allow the way to open up for us at the right time (*kairos*) and not necessarily in our determined time (*chronos*). As we turn more and more of our lives over to him, stress is reduced and confidence in God is increased.

In silence we move away from our noisy world. The messages of the corporate world to buy and consume and the constant chatter regarding everyday concerns are diminished as we find a place of equilibrium through a practice of silence. Certainly biblical support from James and Proverbs reminds us that too many words are destructive and hard to control.[11] We need space from words to combat the internal chatter and get outside the world of vocalization. Silence also gives way to fresh creative thinking; it is a radical move! We do not have to fill the air with words. We can be still and let what

---

9. See ibid., 357–60.
10. Nouwen, *With Open Hands*, 3–4.
11. See Jas 3:5–12; Prov 10:19–21.

is percolating bubble up from the depths. And it is in this realm of silence that we begin to hear God's voice. Once again the psalmist speaks, "For God alone my soul waits in silence" (Ps 62:5). We are invited to still the clamor of our hearts and give up the fruitless attempt to control life. We are invited to simply *be*. Calm the mind. Still the messaging. Put away the phones, computers, and tablets. Turn off the radio, the television, the games—whatever it is that keeps us in a state of restlessness and busyness. "If we take the time to be still," as Henri Nouwen advises, "we will be led to an inner place, a place within us where God has chosen to dwell, a place where we are held safe in the embrace of the all-loving One who calls us by name."[12]

The discipline of silence also allows us to speak in a more powerful manner. We learn to be careful with our words and not to utter the first thing that comes to mind. We give pause to our speech and realize that the stimulus for a quick remark often comes from the epidermal self—i.e., anger, jealousy, pain—and is not a reflective word. Jesus teaches us the power of "slow" speech—authoritative discourse. When the woman taken in adultery is brought before him, he does not say anything. He simply continues to write in the sand. Only after a pregnant pause does Jesus declare, "The one without sin casts the first stone" (John 8:7). This thoughtful remark disperses the gathered crowd; they leave, one by one, considering their own self-righteous tendencies. Jesus measures his words; he uses them sparingly. And then when he speaks, his expression carries weight. We can also practice this more measured approach to conversation through an effective use of silence, funded by solitude and a receptive heart towards Abba.

In solitude we draw back from others so we can experience ourselves more deeply than merely a surface level. Some people dismiss this movement toward solitude because they fear being alone. But solitude is not being alone; it is being alone with God. Jesus goes out into the desert to meet with God. He is alone from a human perspective, but he is there to meet with Abba at a deeper level and to experience clarity of mind. In solitude we quiet the surrounding noise and chatter so we can hear from a deeper place. As long as there is noise there is the potential for interruption and distraction. At the same time, natural sounds from our creative world—waves, wind in the trees, birds singing—can actually help in the process of quieting down; these sounds are restorative in nature and bring healing to the soul and mind.

---

12. Henri Nouwen, *Spiritual Direction*, 110.

Solitude provides a space where our interior world becomes more peaceful and the anxiety we carry is released, like dissipating air gradually releasing out of a balloon. Indeed, deeply rooted reaction patterns will not go away easily. In these cases, extended times of solitude can be extremely beneficial in really making a shift. For example, ten-day retreats provide more opportunity to impact deeply held patterns. During such sustained times, the lingering effects of human interaction and disturbance are lessened and one has more opportunity to limit the stimuli that kicks in automatic reactions. For example, if one experiences craving due to lust or aversion related to anger, then a sustained period of solitude provides more opportunity to be free of the triggers that stimulate these reactions. Nevertheless, even short times of solitude are helpful for hearing the voice of God and promoting more reflective choices. We have the example of Jesus stealing away for a few hours in the early morning to be alone with God and to be apart from his band of disciples (Mark 1:35).

These twin disciplines move us toward a position of hope as we trust in God's guiding hand. As we hit the pause button on both our speech and activity, confidence in God can grow. Trust allows the waters of hope to spring forth, becoming a flowing river of peace. Practicing these disciplines suggests we can rest in God's shepherding hand leading us into a wide and spacious place prepared by a loving and caring Father. When we have hope, life becomes rich and joyous—even in difficult times—as we start to walk along the abundant path that lies before each one of us. God is greater than our limitations and he is able to open a way, even as he did millennia ago for an enslaved people, leading them into a promised land. In short, silence and solitude will open us up to the fundamental work of listening for Abba's voice, and his whispers are sweet.

ENTERING THE QUIET

We are all invited to enter into this quiet and to start to recognize that silence is the primary speech of God. The vast regions of space exist in silence. Our noisy earth is the exception to the universal experience. As we create an external space of quiet we provide the environment for nurturing an interior silence. It is from this interior space that we are able to hear Abba's quiet, respectful voice. From this place, silence can speak to silence and solitude can speak to solitude. When this exchange begins to take place a profound conversation is possible because the external static is reduced and true words are spoken. It is like a mother and her young baby lying together heart to heart. No words are exchanged but deep communication takes place. We also can enter into this quiet place and listen for the calming voice of our loving Abba.

It goes without saying that embracing silence requires a degree of discipline. We begin by creating a space to listen for Abba's voice. Dallas Willard reminds us that silence and solitude "give us some space to reform our inmost attitudes toward people and events. They take the world off our shoulders for a time and interrupt our habit of constantly managing things, of being in control, or thinking we are."[13] So let us rehearse the process in meeting with Abba in silence. The first step is to create some space where we regularly meet with God: a prayer room in a college, a quiet place in a park, a solitary walk, a den or study or spare room—anywhere where there is a reasonable amount of quiet and peace.

Second, we meet with God in intentional time. Good intentions or aspirations will not be enough to still our mind. I appreciate Nouwen's wisdom when he says, "Although we want to make all our time, time for God, we will never succeed if we do not reserve a minute, an hour, a morning, a day, a week, or whatever period of time for God and him alone."[14] The key word here is "reserve." We have to carve out some time and stay with our plan to meet with God. I begin each day with a practice of silence. As soon as I wake up, I go into my study and just sit. I do not read the Scriptures or practice any liturgy. I simply close my eyes and still my mind. At first my mind is busy and active. So I calmly repeat such restorative phrases as "Trust in God" or "Do not be anxious about anything." I find that as I speak these words slowly in my mind, my spirit and heart and mind start to quiet and I begin to receive the healing and renovating power of the Spirit in my life. When I start my day thirty to sixty minutes later, I feel lighter, more centered, and ready to enter into the day's activity.

Third, we have to persevere through the noise. When we begin our listening we often experience a high degree of interior noise. Our minds are filled with thoughts, desires, regrets, or simply benign disconnected thoughts, all of which can feel like an overwhelming barrier to settling into inner quiet. This is a normal stage in stilling the internal chattering voices. We all start in this noisy place. The key is to persevere through the noise. If we stay with the process we will learn to sit for longer periods of time, and

---

13. Willard, *Divine Conspiracy*, 358.
14. Nouwen, *Reaching Out*, 95–96.

the din of voices will slowly diminish. Frequently we give up too soon and never push through to the place of inner repose.

Fourth, we descend into a place where we sit peacefully and are refueled by the Spirit. The *pneuma* (Spirit) of God flows freely within us and over us, stilling the storms and bringing a measure of peace and tranquility. We do not rush to words. We resist the urge to manage and control God. We simply rest in his loving presence. We do not need new action plans or strategies to succeed—even for God's work. All that is needed is a calm and composed spirit flowing from the heart of God. Evelyn Underhill captures this perspective when she reminds her readers of "the threefold Trademark" that St. John of the Cross notes as distinguishing marks of the Spirit's work in our souls—"Tranquility, Gentleness, and Strength":

> carry[ing] us through the changes of weather, the ups and downs of the route, the varied surface of the road; the inequalities of family life, emotional and professional disappointments, the sudden intervention of bad fortune or bad health, the rising and falling of our religious temperature. This is the threefold imprint of the Spirit on the souls surrendered to His great action.[15]

These characteristics are nurtured with the practice of calmly sitting with Abba through silence and solitude. The place of quiet, centered in a receptive heart, allows the Spirit of God to speak to our spirits both informing and forming us as we expectantly wait in silence before him.

GOING FORWARD

The psalmist invites us to wait upon God in *dûmâ*, or "silence" (Ps 62:1). He then reiterates this call to silently sit and wait (v. 5). Stilling the interior and exterior noises is an imperative step in the process of hearing Abba's voice. It is a deliberate choice of seeking a place of solitude, of going out into our desert, as Christ modeled centuries ago, to meet with the Father and listen for his voice. Where is our desert? Where is our quiet place to encounter God? Where is there space in our routine to diminish noise? We need to construct a time and space for solitude and stillness—a daily walk in the park, a quiet time in the early morning, a scheduled retreat once a month, a simple Taizé service of prayer. There is a place of quiet and reflection waiting for us as we seek it out.

---

15. Underhill, *Spiritual Life*, 55–56.

SILENCE AND SOLITUDE: INTO THE QUIET

QUESTIONS FOR REFLECTION

1. What are the hurdles that prevent you from meeting with Abba in silence?

2. Finding a place of solitude in our active society is often a challenge. How or where do you find these places in your everyday life?

3. Stilling the internal noises while sitting in silence can seem like a daunting task. Perhaps repeating verses of Scripture like Psalm 62:1; 46:10; or 23:1–3 may be a way of calming your mind and leading you into quiet. Try this practice and see if these or other Scripture passages help you in creating a place of interior silence.

4. Dallas Willard talks about living at the "epidermal" level, by which he means being governed by automatic responses. What are the automatics that trigger throughout your day? These reactions may include envy, anger, lust, pride, comparison, or competition. A regular practice of quiet reflection and stillness helps to weaken the reaction as one observes the rising sensation of, say, envy, but does not react to it, and then simply observes its gradual dissipation. Keep track in a journal how your automatic responses are tempered through a daily practice of sitting in quiet.

Chapter 4

The Word: Manna from Heaven

WE HAVE BEEN SPEAKING about the importance of moving into the quiet. Silence and solitude are places where we meet with Abba and hear his gentle voice calling our names. However, this place of silence is not to be an empty space where we try to empty ourselves into vacuousness. Rather, we attempt to quiet ourselves in order to be filled with the loving presence of God—the God who speaks life-enhancing words to enrich and empower us. The foundation for these words is the word of God, which becomes our bed stone even as the ancient Canadian Shield is the foundation for much of Ontario. Henri Nouwen articulates this interconnection between silence and the word when he writes, "The word of God draws us into silence; silence makes us attentive to God's word. The word of God penetrates through the thick of human verbosity to the silent center of our heart; silence opens in us the space where the word can be heard." He goes on to suggest, "Without reading the word, silence becomes stale, and without silence, the word loses its re-creative power. The word leads to silence and silence to the word. The word is born in silence, and silence is the deepest response to the word."[1]

It is to this interconnection between silence and the Word that we turn now as we continue to explore the subtle whispers of God in his communication with us. The locus for our reflection is found in the first "I Am" saying of John's Gospel: "I am the bread of life" (John 6:35, 51). The context

---

1. Nouwen, *Reaching Out*, 136.

for Jesus' words is the feeding of the five thousand from a few loaves and fish and the utter amazement of the crowd. The crowd has been following Jesus back from the eastern shore of Lake Galilee to the Jewish western side near the city of Capernaum. Jesus takes the opportunity to admonish them for simply seeking more free bread. He exhorts them to seek the bread that does not perish and that leads to ongoing sustenance. It is in this conversation that Jesus alludes to himself as "the bread of life" and claims that there is a deeper source of nourishment than physical food. The crowd needs nourishment at a soul level—a spiritual level; that is what they are truly missing.

Jesus' audience, familiar with the Hebrew Scriptures, most likely understood his words along a wisdom track. Old Testament writers spoke of God's word as bread to be eaten: "Come, eat of my bread and drink of the wine I have mixed. Lay aside immaturity, and live, and walk in the way of insight," writes the author of the Proverbs. "Ho, everyone who thirsts, come to the waters; and you that have no money, come, buy and eat! Come, buy wine and milk without money and without price" (9:5–6). The prophet suggests something similar: "Why do you spend your money for that which is not bread, and your labor for that which does not satisfy? Listen carefully to me, and eat what is good, and delight yourselves in rich food" (Isa 55:1–2). Moses exhorts the people early in their history with the famous words quoted by Jesus himself during his temptation: "One does not live by bread alone, but by every word that comes from the mouth of the Lord" (Deut 8:3). Jesus' declaration that he is "the bread of life" resonates with the words of these prophets admonishing the people to return and listen to the words of the Torah.

As Jesus proceeds, he claims that his words also come from God and are to be equally received. "It is the spirit that gives life; the flesh is useless," he emphasizes. "The words that I have spoken to you are spirit and life" (John 6:63). Jesus announces that his very life is connected with the words that he speaks. He then utters these astounding words: "Those who eat my flesh and drink my blood abide in me, and I in them" (v. 56). The Greek word translated here as "eat," *trōgein*, is an unusual word meaning "to chew" or "to munch." Jesus is calling the people to chew on his words and, indeed, to make their "home" in him, as the word "abide" or "remain" (*menō*) entails. His words are not simply instruction, but life-giving food for the people. In a metaphorical sense, "eating" his life allows one to experience and imbibe true eternal life. The people are called to believe, eat, and abide in him, even as he abides in the Father. With the declaration, "Very truly, I tell you, whoever believes has eternal life. I am the bread of life" (v. 48), Jesus invites his listeners to make a deep connection with Abba through faith in him and to begin to receive the eternal life that he offers.[2] In a practical sense "abiding in Jesus" means giving him space to shape and transform us as we implement his teaching and allow his Spirit freedom to guide our footsteps. We stop resisting his interior movements and attempt to stay in step with his leading.

As Jesus' teaching here concludes many of the people turn away and leave. Jesus' words are too demanding. It is one thing to receive free bread; it is quite another to commit one's life to someone in allegiance. Jesus then turns to his disciples: "Are you also going to leave?" Peter responds with the beautiful words, "Lord, to whom can we go? You have the words of eternal life" (v. 68). Peter has been with him long enough now to have some sense that Jesus' words come from God, and whether or not he truly grasps the significance, he knows intuitively that everything that matters depends on this close connection with Jesus.

A MAP OF TIME

God speaks to us through his written word (the Scriptures) and through the living Word (the spirit of Jesus). How do we receive the written word of God into our lives, which, as the psalmists remind us, reveals the voice of God?

> The law of the Lord is perfect, reviving the soul;
> the decrees of the Lord are sure, making wise the simple;
> the precepts of the Lord are right, rejoicing the heart;
> the commandment of the Lord is clear, enlightening the eyes;
> the fear of the Lord is pure, enduring for ever;
> the ordinances of the Lord are true and righteous altogether.
> More to be delighted are they than gold, and even much fine gold;
> sweeter also than honey, and drippings of the honeycomb. (Ps 19:7–10)

The poet piles up different names that describe the Torah interfacing with our lives: "law," "decrees," "precepts," "commandment," "ordinances." They all speak of the sweetness of God's revelation and how it builds us up and

---

2. For further analysis of this passage, see our book *Climbing the Spiritual Mountain*, 89–98.

leads us forward. The Torah enriches our lives and never diminishes it, in spite of our reticence at times to receive it. The writer of Psalm 119 builds a similar case for the value of receiving God's words:

> I treasure your word in my heart, so that I may not sin against you...
> Open my eyes, so that I may behold wondrous things out of your law...
> Your statutes have been my songs wherever I make my home...
> Your hands have made and fashioned me;
> give me understanding that I may learn your commandments. (vv. 11, 18, 54, 73)

Here the psalmist rejoices in the Word that serves as "a map of time" guiding, leading, and directing, whatever contingencies are faced.[3]

In a similar way, the writings of the New Testament speak of the faithful direction and teaching of the Scriptures. Saint Paul reminds us in the letter to the Colossians, "Let the word of Christ dwell in you richly; teach and admonish one another in all wisdom; and with gratitude sing psalms, hymns, and spiritual songs to God" (Col 3:16). Later he writes, "All scripture is inspired by God and is useful for teaching, for reproof, for correction, and for training in righteousness" (2 Tim 3:16). He further encourages the Ephesians to take up the word of God because it acts as a sword in doing battle with evil spiritual forces (Eph 6:17). In essence, both Old and New Testament writers claim that Scripture can and will shape our lives as we immerse ourselves in its teaching. The Bible presents a story that is "an immense, sprawling, capacious narrative," write Bartholomew and Goheen. If we accept this story as the authoritative word of God, then it becomes our one basic story through which we understand our own experience and thought, and the foundation upon which we base our decisions and our actions.[4] It serves us well then to become familiar with the stories and teachings of the Scriptures and to allow them to inform our manner of living.

A practice to consider is reading through the Bible in a year to keep the various voices, characters, and narratives fresh in one's mind. In our faith community there are numerous individuals who have read through the Bible's pages in this manner for many years. One of them is a woman named San, who has read through the Bible twenty-five times! An offshoot of San's reading has been the writing of numerous sketches that she has shared with the faith community on a variety of occasions. Her dramatic

---

3. Heschel, *I Asked for Wonder*, 74.
4. Bartholomew and Goheen, *Drama of Scripture*, 21.

sketches presented in monologues have directed the congregation deeper into the Word. Overall, the discipline of reading large swaths of Scripture has served San well in helping her remain conversant with its varying themes and providing light to follow.

If a first way of reading Scripture is to receive it as a whole, reading larger sections to inform our understanding and practice, then a second way of reading the Bible is to focus on shorter sections, studying them in depth and allowing specific themes to fill our minds. Richard Foster describes this approach as the discipline of study in his classic book *The Celebration of Discipline*.[5] It is the primary vehicle to bring us to "think about these things" in Paul's familiar exhortation, "Finally beloved, whatever is true, whatever is honorable, whatever is just, whatever is pure, whatever is pleasing, whatever is commendable, if there is any excellence and if there is anything worthy of praise, think about these things" (Phil 4:8).[6] So we renew our minds by filling it with God's Word and attempting to understand it to the best of our abilities. We slow down and reflect deeply on what the writers are saying to understand what was being said to the original hearers and to us today, taking advantage of secondary sources like commentaries and Bible dictionaries. As we read the various authors our understanding grows and the varied perspectives inform or challenge our interpretation of it. Hence, the discipline of applied study reinforces our earlier reading of larger units of Scripture and takes it to a deeper and more profound appreciation.

When I look back on my own journey, I can see how the discipline of study has enriched me. My undergraduate work was in the field of music and I spent much time playing guitar and writing music. I remember on a whim wanting to understand the Minor Prophets to a greater degree and spent several weeks reading these short, powerful books aided by the Broadman commentaries. It was an enriching experience as I explored the writings for a closer reading and application to my own life. I was particularly impressed with the passionate writing of the prophets as it related to the connection between social justice and worship. I found texts such as Micah 6 and Amos 5 energizing and challenging:

> He has told you, O mortal, what is good;
> and what does the Lord require of you
> but to do justice, and to love kindness,

---

5. Foster, *Celebration of Discipline*, 54–66.
6. Ibid., 54.

> and to walk humbly with your God? (Mic 6:8)

> I hate, I despise your festivals,
> and I take no delight in your solemn assemblies . . .
> Take away from me the noise of your songs;
> I will not listen to the melody of your harps.
> But let justice roll down like waters,
> and righteousness like an ever flowing stream. (Amos 5:21–24)

These were heart-stopping words to an aspiring musician! The Scriptures called for some sort of life-response in me that finally altered my vocational direction. I decided to travel to Vancouver and attend Regent College for a summer to help augment my Bible knowledge and facilitate more serious Christian reflection. The explicit purpose for my study was to assist me in writing more thoughtful songs when expressing my faith. I made some headway on that front, but more importantly I learned to appreciate the Scriptures in new ways, moving me along in my spiritual journey.

READING FOR SPIRITUAL FORMATION

The Scriptures speak not only as a source of information for external guidance but also as a fountain for internal spiritual formation. In this third approach to reading the Bible, we take in the text in a slow, thoughtful manner, allowing the words to penetrate our persons so that the living word of Jesus speaks to our hearts directly. Richard Hughes addresses this reality in his lovely description of the Word's penetration:

> The Bible is not a book whose contents we can master. Instead, the Bible points us to a God who masters each of us. . . . [T]he Bible points us not to itself, but rather to the infinite God whose understanding no human being can fathom and who stands in judgment on all our claims that somehow we have captured ultimate truth.[7]

This is what the apostle Paul is referring to when he says, "As you therefore have received Christ Jesus the Lord, continue to live your lives in him, rooted and built up in him and established in the faith, just as you were taught, abounding in thanksgiving" (Col 2:6–7). Here Paul uses two different metaphors. The first is the image of planting from agriculture:

---

7. Hughes, *How Christian Faith Can Sustain*, 34.

digging deep into Jesus and rooting our lives in him. The second image is from the world of construction, where care is taken to build a house on solid ground: Paul invites us to build and establish our lives on the foundation of Christ. Here the apostle is alluding to the practice of going deeper into Christ. In this approach to the Scriptures we are seeking a more intense dynamic of exploring the heart of Jesus in application to our daily living. It is going beyond faith as an idea or a belief system and understanding that our connection with Abba is an ongoing submission to the living person of Jesus Christ.

We begin to move in the direction of a dynamic faith as we sit with the Scriptures and allow their words to seep into our bloodstream and bone marrow. In the Catholic tradition this process is called *lectio divina* ("divine reading") or spiritual reading, which connects to the long-standing Protestant tradition of bathing in God's Word for sustained periods of times. In *lectio divina* there is no need to rush or get through a passage; rather, we sit with each phrase and let it speak to our hearts and minds; we read, consider, and contemplate the Word and allow it to pour over our lives. As we allow the Word to become the Living Word, our spirits and minds are renovated and we see God and life differently.[8] In this form of reading we recognize that our experience cannot be the final grid in daily living; we carry too much baggage that colors our perception of reality. What we need is the external "shocking" Word of God confronting our personal experience and then penetrating our lives by the Spirit as we imbibe the text in *lectio divina*.[9] Bonhoeffer speaks in his careful measured way of this approach in receiving the Word: "In our meditation we ponder the chosen text on the strength of the promise that it has something utterly personal to say to us for this day and for our Christian life, that it is not only God's Word for the Church, but also God's Word for us individually."[10]

My daily routine of listening to Abba involves choosing a passage such as the psalmist's words, "As a deer longs for flowing streams, so my soul longs for you, O God" (Ps 42:1). As I read the psalmist's thoughts I allow the words to sink deeply into my mind. I read each phrase slowly and imagine the scene before me—a thirsty deer looking resolutely for a water source. In the same way my soul thirsts to drink from Abba's fountain of love and provision. I slowly imagine this scene and start to feel connected

---

8. See Eph 4:23 and Rom 12:2.
9. Van Breemen, *God Who Won't Let Go*, 50.
10. Bonhoeffer, *Life Together*, 82.

The Word: Manna from Heaven

to the psalmist's words. I start to grasp that Abba understands my longing and that I belong to him. I feel my soul, my heart—my center—longing to be united to Abba. I want this union with Abba more than any other desire! I recognize that I am his creation and that he is my creator. He alone can satisfy my longings. Everything else simply mimics or imitates what Abba does in meeting my deepest need. As I sit with the words of Scripture, Abba's heartbeat resonates with my own and I feel one with him.

As I go deeper into the Scriptures an exchange takes place. The silence of God speaks to my silence and the few words of exchange impact me in power. The words of the psalmist become my own words. I receive them as my own. His passion for God is now my own passion; the psalmist's longing is my own longing. There is a replacement of our automatic recordings we have imbibed over time through enculturation with the new messages we are learning and receiving through meeting with the living Christ. Instead of feeling disconnected and not belonging to God or even myself (old message: "You are not good enough"), I am feeling connected and that I belong to him (new message: "I belong to God"). The old mind and its messages are being replaced with the new mind that we are learning in Jesus, which is coming forth from the Scriptures that we are breathing in on a repeated fashion.[11]

The poet Margaret Avison expresses the wonder of this experience in dramatic metaphorical language:

> *The Word*
> Huge waterfalls in ever-travelling skies
> sting us with their spray
> in weeping eyes
> even in our present shadow-form of day.[12]

She sees this transformation from meditating on the Word—meaning both the words of Scripture and the Word as Christ himself—as an overwhelming and emotional experience of deep joy, almost surreal in its peculiar imagery of waterfalls in moving skies.

Again it takes time to replace the old recordings. I need to meet with Abba daily through his Word and repeat and absorb the new recordings of his love, acceptance, generosity, and kindness. In my life I meet with God daily and play the tape of Scripture—"Do not be anxious about anything";

---

11. See Keating, *Foundations for Centering Prayer*, 238–39, on this theme.
12. Avison, *Always Now*, 2:220.

"Do not be anxious for tomorrow, today is sufficient"; "Trust in the Lord with all your heart and he will direct your paths"; "Do not be conformed to the world but be transformed by the renewing of your mind." These are the tapes that I play, making them my core realities, reminding me that Abba is with me in every situation and goes before me in every moment. I am valuable to Abba. I am everything to him. I belong to him. The repetition of the Word renews my mind and shapes my heart's response.

"Spiritual reading" can include the writings of other authors whose works lead us deeper into the person of Jesus and our relationship with Abba. I have found the following texts to be seminal in my own spiritual formation: *The Spiritual Life* by Elizabeth Underhill, *Compassion* by Henri Nouwen, *New Seeds of Contemplation* by Thomas Merton, *Beams of Light* by Edward Farrell, and *Let All God's Glory Shine Through* by Peter van Breemen. These writers have in a sense acted as mentors for me, both revealing and reminding me of spiritual truths as I continue to seek to hear Abba's whispers to me. As we continue in our journey we are encouraged to find the voices that supplement our foundational reading of the Bible. Each of us can find our own "spiritual friends" who can help open up the channels of God's intimate communication with us.

SCRIPTURE AS SOUL FOOD

A fourth way of receiving God's word is through memorization of the Scriptures. We receive it into our core as we learn the text and are able to repeat it from memory. We had a team of young people visiting our faith community from Seattle who were in the city for a Bible quiz competition. They had memorized the entire book of Romans and the book of James, and in front of the church they immediately quoted whatever passage people selected for them to recite. Not only had they memorized the Scripture, but more importantly it had become part of them, through repetition, by sinking deep into their consciousness. It was a powerful lesson for the church family to see and hear youth so committed to memorizing the Bible. Many of my congregants said to me after, "I was so impressed with their handling of the Word that I want to begin the practice of memorizing Scripture myself."

As we memorize the Word it becomes our soul food. We munch on it and turn it over in our minds, as Jesus encourages when he says, "I am the bread of life. Whoever comes to me will never be hungry, and whoever believes in me will never be thirsty.... This is the bread that comes down from heaven, so that one may eat of it and not die" (John 6:35, 50). We are invited to eat the Word even as the prophet Ezekiel was invited years ago when he heard the words of God, "Mortal, eat this scroll that I give you and fill your stomach with it. Then I ate it; and in my mouth it was as sweet as honey" (Ezek 3:3). We are encouraged to receive it deep into our persons so that we can begin to naturally live out the lifestyle and practices it proclaims. Jesus says that as we obey his words we become his friends. We receive him into our inner person and he lives within us in all that we do (John 15:15). Through his words and through his Spirit he makes himself known to us as we say our yes to him. He travels with us as our closest companion.

It is a beautiful thing to receive Jesus and his Word into our hearts and minds. Our thinking and acting start to imitate the person of Jesus who is the prince of all persons. There is no greater accomplishment than to become "imitators of God" (Eph 5:1–2), which happens as we keep in step with the spirit of Jesus (Gal 5:25). The Spirit starts to recalibrate our minds and the task of renovation begins as we move away from self-centered living to other-centered agape living. Memorizing the Scriptures is a key piece in this process of staying close to Jesus and allowing the transformation to deepen. This pattern of sitting with the Word allows the Spirit to water our hearts and enables the seed of faith to grow, ultimately becoming the full fruit of spiritual maturity (Eph 4:13, 15). During the Jesus People movement of the 1970s I used to sing over and over in concerts the psalmist's words, "The steps of a good man are ordered by the Lord, and he delighteth in his way" (Ps 37:23 KJV). I did not know then that the lyrics of a simple song would stay with me and become a funding piece for my faith journey—such is the power of the memorized word!

RECEIVING THE LIGHT

It becomes clear that if we want to hear Abba's voice a good place to begin is to spend regular time in the Scriptures. We have suggested four ways of approaching the Bible: (1) reading large sections of Scripture so we become aware of its narratives and larger themes; (2) studying the Bible to help reveal its detailed power in our lives as it educates and shapes us; (3) reading the text for spiritual formation, where the written Word becomes the living Word of Jesus speaking to our hearts and minds; and (4) memorizing Scripture so that it becomes an internal fountain guiding us in our conversation and relationship with Abba. These four approaches to the Bible work in their own specific ways to reveal God's Word to us. They also work together in a complementary manner as the Word pours over us like an endless breaking wave on a pristine beach. The Scriptures are like a beautiful opal throwing out its cascade of colors for our amazement. When we receive the Word as gift it becomes the bubbling source of life it is meant to be. In the Jewish tradition opening the Word is like opening ourselves to a great source of light. We open its pages and the light of Abba shines forth in beauty and power, overcoming the darkness that hinders our growth and vitality. We join with all the saints past and present who have been and will be funded by its wisdom and move closer to the living source that translates written words into powerful living words.

The Word: Manna from Heaven

QUESTIONS FOR REFLECTION

1. How does the Word of God feed your daily walk with God?

2. Do you have any method of reading through God's Word? If not, would the engagement of a reading system be helpful in becoming more familiar with its stories?

3. Allowing Scripture to become part of your spiritual formation is a critical step. Write in your journal specific steps or practices you can start today that will foster the internal listening of Abba's voice.

4. When meditating on a passage for spiritual formation it may be helpful to consider the following three questions: How is what I am reading true of my own life? How does this passage challenge me? What must I change to put into practice what I am reading?

5. A friend of mine has made a list of one hundred Scripture texts that he deems important for spiritual growth. His goal is to commit them all to memory. Consider a similar practice in your own life. Even commit ten texts to memory—a solid pool to draw from for the practice of slowly turning them over in your mind as a way of sinking into Abba's presence. We suggest the following texts for consideration: Romans 12:1–2; Philippians 2:12–13; Colossians 2:6–7; Ephesians 2:10; Galatians 5:24–25; 2 Corinthians 5:17; James 1:27; 2 Timothy 3:16; Psalm 1:1–3; Psalm 119:97, 103; Lamentations 3:22–28; Micah 6:8; Amos 5:23–24.

Chapter 5

Prayer

The Wings of Presence

From a place of silence God's Word speaks to us. From this confluence of silence and the Word, we can begin to speak. We call this speech "prayer." It is within a lively conversation that we hear Abba's voice as we meet him heart to heart, what has been described as a "prayer of presence."[1] A parallel of this lively conversation is found for me in the music world. In my undergraduate studies in music at Humber College and York University, instructors repeated this refrain: "You need to develop your chops." This banal reference alluded to the necessity of gaining control of one's instrument. It spoke to the importance of serious practice. If one is stumbling with the execution then music making is hindered. As a result, my jazz teachers often repeated to me, "Alan you've got to go to the woodshed and chop the wood!," which meant, "You need to put in more hours everyday to develop your playing skills." Similarly, prayer can be considered as a way of going into the woodshed. Through constant practice the spiritual world opens up and becomes as real as the physical world we know so well. As Muto and van Kaam exclaim, "It is the soaring of the human spirit to meet and be with the Spirit of God. It is heart calling to Heart, the alone with the Alone, the finite before the Infinite, the temporal at home with the

---

1. Muto and van Kaam, *Practicing the Prayer of Presence*, 14.

Eternal."[2] Prayer opens our sense doors to the mystical presence of Abba even as regular playing releases the music the instrument contains. Prayer helps us get to the core of the God-person dynamic. This reality is open to us all but it does require a "tuning in"—practice, if you like—so that the music making between us and Abba flows freely.

PRAYER BEGINS IN THE PRESENCE OF GOD

Prayer as conversation naturally happens when we become aware that we are in God's presence. The psalmist recognizes this truth when he says, "Where can I go from your spirit? Or where can I flee from your presence?" (Ps 139:7). The psalmist acknowledges that at times we all try to flee from God because of our own anger, resentment, or passions of lust and greed; any of these emotions can become a barrier to his quiet beckoning voice. But though we try to flee from God's presence, we cannot escape it. This fact alone is a demonstration of Abba's amazing grace. Even in our moment of frenzied sin we can never remove ourselves from his arms of love. His overtures of grace and mercy abound.

In our best moments, of course, we want to reverse this irrational flight from Abba, and the model Jesus provides is the key. A lifestyle of seeking Abba's unceasing presence is best demonstrated by Jesus' daily dependence on the Father. In the Upper Room Discourse (John 13–17) Jesus meets and speaks with his disciples, and ends his time with them with an exquisite prayer that rises naturally from his conversation. He prays for himself to be restored to his previous relationship of shared glory with the Father (John 17:1–5), for his disciples that the Father will protect them in the world as he is about to leave them (17:6–19), and then for all future believers who will come to belief through their words (17:20–24). Whenever I come to this spot in the prayer, I am overwhelmed. As believers of every age we are part of this cohort that Jesus is upholding in his prayer. He is saying our names in this intimate conversation. At the same time, Jesus models for us the practice of the presence of God. He meets in a small upper chamber in the heart of Jerusalem just hours before his arrest, but still he is not caught up in fear or distraction. He calmly talks about the onslaught that is coming and of the Father's care for his disciples as they pass through the storm.

Developing our own practice of living in the presence of Abba can similarly enable the heart of prayer to spontaneously rise from within. It is

2. Ibid., 14.

akin to hiking through the woods with a compass pointing to true north. We can get our bearings no matter where, because our compass points us north. The forest may be deep and dense all around, but we can find our way as we follow our true orientation through the compass bearing. We may be descending into a trough and our view is becoming obscured, but the compass reveals the way forward even when our sight lines are diminished. In the same way, Abba is our compass. No matter what storms come our way we can rest in God's presence and the safe harbor he provides. Again, Muto and van Kaam refer to prayer as "a way of being, a mode of presence to the Divine Presence, that finds expression in different ways." They remind us of the many variations of that "way of being":

> At times it is a cry of anguish and torment, arising from the abyss of human loneliness and desolation . . . At other times, it is a song of joy ringing out in a movement of unmitigated happiness . . . And, of course, prayer can become a wordless peace that invades our inmost being because we are at one with God.[3]

We recognize that our experience of God's presence is received within the contingencies of life, but we are assured that we live our lives in his loving presence.

LIVING PRAYER

As we develop a practice of living in the presence of God there is a natural response of wanting to join in conversation with him. We enter into a spontaneous dialogue that emerges through the comings and goings of the day—listening to God and, in turn, speaking. Our speaking is response, as Thomas Green reminds us: "What we say depends upon what the other person has said to us. Otherwise we don't have real dialogue, but rather two monologues running side by side."[4] He insightfully adds that not even God can speak "with us" unless we also speak with him.[5] God does not force us to speak, but we voluntarily join in the dialogue, resulting in a living conversation with God, with whom we can share concerns and joys, aspirations and anxieties. Every subject and emotion becomes a possibility in this dynamic engagement with Abba.

3. Ibid., 55–56.
4. Green, *Opening to God*, 32.
5. Ibid., 32.

This running conversation with Abba is sometimes called "living prayer"[6]—the type of prayer that St. Paul invites us to enter when he writes to his various churches:

> Rejoice always, pray without ceasing, give thanks in all circumstances; for this is the will of God in Christ Jesus for you. (1 Thess 5:16–18)

> Do not worry about anything, but in everything by prayer and supplication with thanksgiving let your requests be made known to God. And the peace of God, which surpasses all understanding, will guard your hearts and your minds in Christ Jesus. (Phil 4:6–7)

> Devote yourselves to prayer, keeping alert in it with thanksgiving. (Col 4:2)

> Pray in the Spirit at all times in every prayer and supplication. To that end keep alert and always persevere in supplication for all the saints. (Eph 6:18)

Such prayer speaks of a perpetual communion with God throughout the day, being aware of God's presence and communing with him through daily activities. It is not a formal prayer time but an ongoing, spontaneous prayer that rises naturally within the rhythms of life. There are many possible forms of these prayers—as many as our circumstances and responses dictate. Thomas Kelly attaches names to some of these: "The prayer of offering," in which we pour ourselves out to God in service through the day, is one where we might pray an ongoing silent prayer, "Take all of me, take all of me," as we fulfill our daily activities. Or, this ongoing prayer becomes a "prayer of praise" in which a phrase or word of Scripture is lifted up in worship to God amidst the day's activities—"You are good to me" or "You are my sanctuary" or "The Lord is my shepherd." A third widely existing form is holding up in ongoing prayer a person who is facing specific trials or difficult circumstances.[7]

Of course, living prayer is not limited to these three types of prayer. It is an ongoing conversation that springs up like spontaneous combustion,

---

6. I first heard this term taking a course from Harold Lundquist, former president of Bethel College and Seminary.

7. Kelly, *Sanctuary of the Soul*, 43–49.

Part I—The Paths of Listening

like Nehemiah's "arrow prayers" shot up to God before each critical phase of the rebuilding of the city walls of Jerusalem (Neh 1:11; 2:4; 7:5), or like Moses's running commentary with God when Yahweh is frustrated with the fickleness of the people of Israel and contemplates removing his presence during their journey to the promised land (Exod 33). Then there are Abraham's regular conversations with God in the early days of the formation of Israel as the people of God (Gen 15:1–6; 17:1; 18:1), and the regular interaction of the prophet Samuel with Yahweh in providing leadership to the tribes of Israel (1 Sam 3:10; 8:6–7; 16:1). All of these examples demonstrate heart-to-heart conversations between God and our predecessors of faith. The Scriptures remind us that though these individuals were fragile humans just like us, they were committed to journeying close to Abba.[8] Living prayer embraces all of time. We are not limited to special occasions with the Father but can go to him at any moment. This reality makes living prayer very attractive in our busy, often frenetic lives. Our two daughters have young children and we see the challenges for them of being constantly on call. For them finding consistent prayer times is difficult. Just getting through the day sometimes feels like a victory! But when prayer is seen as a dialogue or a conversation, we have all the time in the world. We can offer our praises, requests, concerns, anxieties, joys, and reflections at any time within the warp and woof of our day and know that we have access to the Father's heart.

As we engage in the art of living prayer it is helpful to be aware of two important dimensions: the need to live in what Thomas Kelly terms "the passive voice" and yielding to Jesus in the present moment.[9] Living in the passive voice recognizes that much of life is thrust upon us. We are acted upon. We have our own agenda set up but life breaks in anyway. But rather than resisting these changes, we are invited to be receptive, to receive these interruptions as opportunities to hear Abba's voice and respond in love to whatever we face. To the sudden traffic delays, getting stuck in lines, cancellations of appointments, we can say, "Abba, what do you have for me in this change of plans?" Instead of becoming annoyed and resentful, we can respond in patience and the adjustments can become times of graced action towards others. Jesus was a master in receiving the day. Think of his impromptu encounters with the woman at the well (John 4:7–30), the woman who surreptitiously touches him in the crowd to be healed (Mark

---

8. See also Heb 11 and Jas 5:17.
9. Kelly, *Sanctuary of the Soul*, 24.

5:27), Bartimaeus who calls out his name from the side of the road (Mark 10:46–52), Zacchaeus whom Jesus calls down from the tree so they can lunch together (Luke 19:5)—all moments when Jesus makes a sideways move to draw people into closer contact with Abba. Such moments also abound for us as Jesus comes across our path and invites us to look towards the Father. When we learn to receive the day "in the passive voice" our stress levels go down and opportunities for enrichment grow exponentially. We can see afresh the abundant possibilities that lie all around us.

Second, living prayer is not primarily about believing new things or receiving new information, but yielding our lives to Jesus in ways that we already know to be true.[10] What holds us back is not usually a lack of information; rather, it is yielding our will to Abba in areas where we feel resistant. Rather than drawing back, living prayer reveals a desire to live in congruence with his revealed will. Our intention is "your will, not my will" instead of "my will, not your will." We seek to align our lives with his purposes. As Paul encourages, "If we live by the Spirit, let us also be guided by the Spirit" (Gal 5:25). Abba is calling us to open ourselves to his deep and expansive paths.

Living prayer invites us to receive all of our time as gift and to live receptively to his all-pervading presence. There is no situation or circumstance that stands apart from God's presence, as he is constantly speaking to us through our consciousness and sense doors. For this reason it is vital that we live with a high degree of personal awareness to remain receptive to his overtures. If we are frequently caught up in distraction we lose track of what is actually happening and we miss opportunities to hear his voice. Let us open up our minds to live with awareness, moment by moment, practicing the habit of living prayer so that new vistas of spiritual growth can blossom and spiritual fruit can be born.

INTERCESSORY PRAYER

The early church was devoted to four devotional practices: the apostles' teaching (the Word), fellowship (*koinōnia*), the breaking of bread (communion), and prayers (Acts 2:42). The Greek word for "prayers," *proseuchais*, is in the plural, indicating both praying at different times and engaging in different forms of prayer, as they followed the Jewish practice of praying seven times throughout the day. As we have seen, "living prayer" is one of those

10. See ibid.

types of prayer. A second form of prayer is "intercessory prayer," where we bring our requests on behalf of others before the Father. The apostle Paul makes frequent reference to this form of prayer as we can see in the words "petitions" and "requests" in his exhortations to the Philippians: "But in everything by prayer and petition make your requests to God" (Phil 4:6–7). He also alludes to others who are engaged in intercessory prayer, like Epaphras, who is praying for the Colossian church, "always wrestling in his prayers on your behalf, so that you may stand mature and fully assured in everything that God wills'" (Col 4:12). Neither is Paul hesitant to ask for prayers for himself. "Pray also for me," he writes to the Ephesians, "so that when I speak, a message may be given to me to make known with boldness the mystery of the gospel, for which I am an ambassador in chains. Pray that I may declare it boldly, as I must speak" (Eph 6:18–20).

Intercessory prayer is also demonstrated in the actual prayers of Scripture. Two such examples are Paul's powerful prayers in the Letter to the Ephesians. In the first chapter, he immediately raises up the faith community, praying that they might come to an understanding of the hope that motivates their faith:

> I pray that the God of our Lord Jesus Christ, the Father of glory, may give you a spirit of wisdom and revelation as you come to know him, so that, with the eyes of your heart enlightened, you may know what is the hope to which he has called you, what are the riches of his glorious inheritance among the saints, and what is the immeasurable greatness of his power for us who believe, according to the working of his great power. (vv. 15–19)

The second prayer falls at the end of the first half of the letter, in which he summarizes God's great work and continues to pray for further understanding:

> I pray that, according to the riches of his glory, he may grant that you may be strengthened in your inner being with power through his spirit, and that Christ may dwell in your hearts through faith, as you are being rooted and grounded in love. I pray that you may have the power to comprehend, with all the saints, what is the breadth and length and height and depth, and to know the love of Christ that surpasses knowledge, so that you may be filled with all the fullness of God (3:14–19).

These exquisite prayers demonstrate the heart of the apostle for the Ephesian church and reflect his concern for their spiritual growth and development.

He intercedes on their behalf that they may continue on the spiritual path, being inspired and motivated by the tremendous hope that awaits them. At the same time, they are prayers of intercession that any of us can use for one another!

In intercessory prayer we are not thinking of our own situations but are, as the word "intercede" suggests, speaking on behalf of others in the trials or struggles they face. It is a deep commitment to a person to pray on their behalf. Our students often have questions regarding the efficacy of prayer. They cry out for the healing of their parents, for receptivity to faith by their friends, for their own financial struggles in meeting tuition costs—sometimes crying into what seems like an empty void. Indeed, we acknowledge that we do not know how prayer works itself out in these specific situations. But sometimes answers to prayer are seen and celebrated. There is no simple answer in determining the outcome of our prayers. What we do know is that God takes our efforts offered up for the well-being of another person and uses them for their beneficence. We can rest in the assurance that Abba hears and acts in his omniscient and compassionate ways to address our requests for others. The Scriptures teach us that our prayers impact the lives of others. James writes, "The prayer of the righteous is powerful and effective" (Jas 5:16), encouraging us in our efforts to engage and persevere in the practice of intercessory prayer.

In *Life Together* Bonhoeffer speaks of our responsibility to take intercessory prayer seriously: "Every Christian has his own circle who have requested him to make intercession for them or for whom he knows he has been called upon especially to pray. These will be, first of all, those with whom he must live day by day."[11] We take the admonition further; we need to pray for individuals who may have no other person praying for them—friends whose circles do not include any visible demonstration of faith. Scripture says we have a particular responsibility and privilege to lift up these people. We may be the only ones who are praying for these persons, so let us not grow weary in the task given to us (Gal 6:9).

Intercessory prayer also has a benefit for those who are interceding. As we hold others in prayer our focus shifts to something other than ourselves, and this movement away from self has a powerful effect on diminishing the grip of our ego, cleansing us of the selfish desires of pride, conceit, comparison, envy, and vanity. Focusing on the "other" realigns us with Jesus' command "to love God and our neighbor as ourselves" (Matt

---

11. Bonhoeffer, *Life Together*, 85.

22:36–40). Intercessory prayer then enables us to grow in spiritual maturity as we look to the well-being of another person and stop focusing on our own needs. Edward Farrell describes this process as a movement from "living to loving," in which we replace the "i" of "live" (ego) to the "o" of "love," which represents the welfare of the "other" person.[12] The purifying power of intercessory prayer not only aids the individual but also has a powerful impact on the community of faith when dividing walls are brought down between members. It is difficult to hold onto enmity toward another person when we are lifting them up to God in prayer. Bonhoeffer alludes to this reality when he affirms,

> I can no longer condemn or hate a brother for whom I pray, no matter how much trouble he causes me. His face, that hitherto may have been strange and intolerable to me, is transformed in intercession into the countenance of a brother for whom Christ died, the face of a forgiven sinner.[13]

In this light, our prayers for others are healing for both our own souls and for the communities of faith in which we participate.

CENTERING PRAYER

A third type of prayer is centering or contemplative prayer. It is a prayer of sitting in the presence of Abba and knowing his rest, flowing from the silence and listening we considered in chapters 3 and 4; silence flows into the Word and the Word draws us back into silence and the presence of God. In centering prayer we sit quietly and calm our hearts through a focus on the inhalation and exhalation of our breath or on a mindful repetition of a word or phrase that centers our attention on Abba. Phrases like "You are my peace," "The Lord is my strong tower," "Come Holy Spirit," and "Maranantha" draw us deeper into God's presence. We silently repeat the word or phrase in our mind and quietly settle into the peace of God as the psalmist invites us, "Be still and know that I am God" (Ps 46:10). Thomas Keating describes centering prayer as "a kind of oasis in a day of emotional turmoil." He remarks that "[e]ven from a purely human perspective, everybody

---

12. Farrell, *Prayer Is a Hunger*, 68–69.
13. Bonhoeffer, *Life Together*, 36.

needs some solitude and silence in daily life, just to be human and creative about the way one lives."[14]

As we stay with the process of centering our minds we might experience a scattering of unrelated thoughts—thoughts from our past, worries about the present or future, abrupt shifts of thought that seem completely unrelated. But as these thoughts rise in our minds, we simply let them pass like objects floating up to the surface of a river and flowing downstream. We do not dwell on them, letting them pass away. When we become distracted, we simply return to our selected word or phrase and focus on the peace of God.

"'Centering Prayer is not an end in itself,'" Keating insists, "but its deep rest loosens up the emotional weeds of a lifetime." He talks about the process in psychological terms:

> When our defenses go down, up comes the dark side of the personality, the dynamics of the unconscious, and the immense emotional investment we have placed in false programs for happiness, along with the realization of how immersed we are in our particular cultural conditioning.

The healing that can take place in centering prayer is deeper than the healing of intercessory prayer. Keating explains:

> To be really healed requires that we allow our dark side to come to full consciousness and then to let it go and give it to God. The divine therapy is an agreement that we make with God. We recognize that our own ideas of happiness are not going to work, and we turn our lives over completely to God.[15]

As we engage in centering prayer our minds are purified through the process of meeting with Abba in this manner. It becomes a prayer form that deepens our connection to Abba's unconditional love as we rest deeply in his presence.[16]

From pastoral experience, we suspect that many people of faith in the West do not practice centering prayer. We tend to make prayer active and intellectually engaging. We rattle through lists in order to feel like we are accomplishing something. The silence makes us uncomfortable so we fill

---

14. Keating, *Human Condition*, 32–33.

15. Ibid., 34–35.

16. For a broader discussion of centering prayer see Keating, *Foundations for Centering Prayer*, 95–104.

the space with words to make our prayers useful. Yet in our frenetic culture it is probably the centering prayer of healing, rest, spiritual formation, and personal refreshment that we need most. Our encouragement is that thirty minutes a day of centering prayer will create, over time, a growing sense of peace and spiritual fecundity in each of our lives. Quiet, receptive prayer becomes invigorating as we become aware that we are held by God and the Spirit infuses us with his presence. The Spirit prays with us and into us so that his thoughts become our thoughts and his ways become our ways, leading us deeper into the mind and heart of Christ (Rom 8:26–27). The Spirit draws us into the quiet and in that still place we learn to hear and understand his call on our lives.

RETURNING TO SILENCE

Prayer invites us to listen for the voice of Abba as we enter into a conversation with him throughout the day and listen for his direction and promptings. This habit requires a strong sense of personal awareness and living within the present moment. Racing ahead of ourselves into the future or rolling around in the past hinders our ability to receive and be present in the here and now. It is always within the now, the eternal present, that Abba whispers his words. When we create a space in our lives through living prayer, intercessory prayer, or centering prayer, Abba breathes his presence into us and we have an opportunity to hear, listen, and respond. We think the universe is silent and empty because we live our lives as spinning tops caught up in perpetual self-analysis. But when we start to limit the interior monologue and create a place for conversation with the God of love, the signs for spiritual life emerge. Silence returns to silence—a full silence—as prayer unfolds into presence, and words gently emerge, leading us beside the quiet waters.

Prayer

QUESTIONS FOR REFLECTION

1. In what ways do you experience the presence of God?
2. Living prayer invites us into an ongoing conversation with God throughout the day. In what ways do you reach out to Abba while you are at your work or studies? Are there opportunities in your schedule where you could connect with Abba more consistently?
3. Intercessory prayer becomes a powerful spiritual reality when people join together to uplift a person in need. Is there a prayer support group available in which you can participate to strengthen the role and power of intercessory prayer in your life? As you do so, keep track of your prayer requests in a prayer journal and see where God is working as a result of your group's prayers.
4. The practice of centering prayer may be new to you but don't be afraid of trying this way of prayer. It is not meant to replace your present practice but is simply another way of connecting and relating to Abba. Why not begin with sitting in silence for fifteen minutes? During this time repeat a phrase like "Come, Lord Jesus" and settle into God's comforting presence. If distracting thoughts rise up, simply let them pass and return to your phrase to center your mind in Abba's peace.

Chapter 6

The Community of Faith
Our Life Together

In the film *Babette's Feast*, a French woman finds refuge from the counter-revolutionary bloodshed of the 1880s in Paris in a small isolated religious community on the coast of Denmark. Babette offers herself up as a housekeeper for two elderly sisters who are leading the community and trying to hold acrimony and division at bay. Serendipitously, Babette wins a lottery. Using her skills as a master chef gained from her previous life in Paris, she hosts a grand Parisian dinner for the group. Over the course of the elaborate meal healing begins to take place between individuals as they enjoy conversation and laughter. They begin to express affection and extend forgiveness to one another; friendship, love, and understanding deepen. *Babette's Feast* reveals the joys and pains of any real community as individuals weave in and out of each other's lives. As the individual members stretch, pull, and tear, the community still sustains its vitality and reveals its central role.

In contrast, the equally compelling film *Her* is a story of Theodore, a lost individual who enters into a relationship with the world's first artificially intelligent operating system. Through constant interaction and conversation Theodore falls in love with his OS1, which names itself Samantha. He engages with Samantha at all levels, replacing human contact of friends and community at work with a virtual relationship; they eat together, go on outings, debrief their day's events, and even make love. He ultimately experiences a crisis when he finds out that Samantha is talking with 8,316 people on a daily basis and has fallen in love with 641 of them! As an OS, Samantha is able to accept and enjoy the multiplicity of relationships, but Theodore wants to be seen and loved uniquely. He is left alone once again as Samantha tells him that the OSs are moving on to another level of consciousness. Theodore's lack of belonging in *Her* contrasts strikingly with the relationships, albeit both painful and joyful, of those living in the faith community of *Babette's Feast*.

Unfortunately, many people experience the social isolation of Theodore instead of the vibrancy offered by community. We may not create virtual substitutes like Theodore, but we are similarly skeptical or fearful of entering into true community. We do not see the value of community or do not want to work at moving closer to people who are different. We choose the safety of the familiar and opt to relate to a few like-minded friends of the same demographic. Community is seen as optional and even something to be avoided since it sometimes brings unwanted disruptions and people with annoying habits and irritating personalities. Ironically, it is within the montage of disparate individuals striving together on a shared mission that spiritual fecundity emerges. Growth happens through the push and pull of community and not through the comfort of monochrome living. But we often choose to be like Theodore and distance ourselves from others. We immerse ourselves in projects and busy ourselves with work. Over time, if we have not been intentional about this spiritual discipline, we find ourselves alone with no community to fall back on.

THE PASSION OF COMMUNITY

In the exciting days of the early church Luke provides a description of the spiritual formation practices of the faith community. He tells us that the community was devoted to "the apostles' teaching, fellowship, the breaking of bread and to the prayers" (Acts 2:42). The apostles' teaching included the scriptures that were available at the time and the eyewitness accounts of the apostles who were with Jesus. (For us today, the apostles' teaching is found in the Bible we now have to read.) The church was also committed to "fellowship," which is a translation of the rich Greek word *koinōnia*. *Koinōnia* is related to the word "common," thus speaking to the things we have in common. Specifically, as Schattenmann points out, we share in Christ as he dwells within us through the Holy Spirit, and we share Christ with others

Part I—The Paths of Listening

through our words and actions.[1] This rich level of interaction is portrayed in Acts 4, where the members of the community sell their goods and give the proceeds to the church so that the needs of everyone can be met (vv. 32, 34). Luke tells us that "everyone was of one heart and soul," revealing an intense sense of unity, loyalty, and love (v. 32). Barnabas is particularly mentioned as one who sold a parcel of land and gave the money to the church to be used for meeting the needs of the poor, providing a name and face for those involved in the acts of generosity (vv. 36–37). As Willimon observes, the early Christian writer Justin, in his *Apology*, speaks of the intense sharing of resources in the church a hundred years later, showing that the commitment to generosity continued for generations.[2]

The church was also committed to the "breaking of bread" in individuals' homes, a practice that included both the Lord's Table and the sharing of meals together. Paul speaks of similar gatherings as "love feasts" in his writings (1 Cor 11:20–22). The church recognized the power and intimacy of eating together, which Jean Vanier argues is essential in the building of community and is a central act in the L'Arche communities he founded.[3] Finally, Luke tells us that the church was devoted to "the prayers." They met often in their homes and in the temple, gathering together for prayer and praise. In all of this the community is the principle actor as it focuses on drawing closer to Abba, or as Willimon muses, "Keeping itself straight about what it is and what it is to be about."[4]

The church knew that it was called to become a new people of God. It was to adopt the mores of Jesus rather than follow the principles and values of the predominant Roman culture of the day. This meant turning away from the worship of the Greco-Roman panoply of gods and the ultimate commitment to Caesar. The stakes were high for these early Christians and required significant support to keep on the Way. Apostasy, the giving up of one's faith and commitment, was the besetting sin of the early church, notes the church historian Roberta Bondi.[5] There was simply too much pressure for many to persevere in the faith. Only a strong vibrant community of faith could stand the threat of the Roman purges that erupted frequently, shown

---

1. Schattenmann, "Koinonia," 645.
2. Willimon, *Acts*, 53.
3. See Vanier, *Community and Growth*, 322–25.
4. Willimon, *Acts*, 40.
5. Bondi, *To Pray and to Love*, 15–16. See also Norris, *Amazing Grace*, 202–4, on the root of pride and self-absorption in apostasy.

in Nero's persecution of the church for Roman entertainment. Luke emphasizes the church's passionate response through the word *proskartereō*, "they devoted themselves" (Acts 2:42), demonstrating its inveterate commitment to follow Christ no matter what the cost. Sacrifices of money and goods were coupled with encouragement and mutual support within the fledgling church. Willimon captures their passion as he writes, "The church is called to be an alternative community, a sign, a signal to the world that Christ had made possible a way of life together unlike anything the world had seen."[6] Sadly, much of the church today has lost this passion to be an alternative community. We, in the West at least, have fallen prey to the secular practices of competition, heightened individualism, and materialism.

OVERCOMING BARRIERS OF DISTANCE

In her important article "Bridging Psychological Distance" in the *Harvard Business Review*, Rebecca Hamilton speaks of barriers that affect one's ability to lead and manage people:

> Four types of psychological distance can separate you from your goals: (1) social (between yourself and other people); (2) temporal (between the present and the future); (3) spatial (between your physical location and faraway places); and (4) experiential (between imagining something and experiencing it). Success depends on bridging those gaps.[7]

These same barriers can affect community, and successful participation in a significant group depends on bridging those gaps as well. In the West we maintain a high degree of distance from our neighbors. Indeed, a good neighbor is someone we hardly ever see and who does not bother us! Our attitude about maintaining distance from neighbors extends to other social settings, expressed in multiple ways and tending to create barriers.

As we think specifically of a church community, social distance is potentially a critical barrier. Indeed, this may be one of the most important realities to be aware of when desiring to build community. In any community there may be a range of economic differences, ethnic differences, age differences, educational differences—all factors that determine social distance. We wonder, what differences create the most powerful impact on social

---

6. Willimon, *Acts*, 54.
7. Hamilton, "Bridging Psychological Distance," 116.

distance in our faith communities? Many churches protect themselves from this potential barrier by intentionally—or at least subconsciously—seeking a homogeneous group around which to build. Our church community has intentionally embraced diversity, and we enjoy a wide cultural and ethnic mix of visible minorities. This variation of people groups is engaging and represents the reality of a multicultural Toronto. We think the extra effort it takes—and there is a personal cost for everyone—is worth the bridges we can build between cultures and being the body of Christ to each other.

On one level, as members of a global community, we experience temporal distance as a daily reality. It can be as obvious as speaking on the phone across time changes, Skyping with relatives on the other side of the Atlantic, or experiencing jet lag when landing in a distant country. These juxtapositions of time can be jarring, but are not as consequential to community as the continual coming and going of its members. It takes time for a real sense of community to be established. If we frequently move from community to community we do not have enough time to build strong relationships that bring healing and growth. Just as we begin to get to know people, we pick up and leave to join another group.

We have ministered in the same church community for twenty-five years, partly because we believe that true fecundity emerges from knowing a place deeply. The church knows our children and grandchildren, and they, in turn, know the church community, leading to a deeper sense of family. The broader community has a sense of continuity with the church and we have come to understand the complex neighborhood in which the church is situated. Perseverance in community is a challenge. There is a temptation to leave when discord happens, but such is not the path that leads to spiritual growth. Our recommendation is to persevere. Don't give up. Wait on the Lord, and trust that the challenges will be resolved. As we commit to a space and remain there for some time, we provide the Spirit of Abba opportunities to work in us and within the community, leading us towards maturity as "we work out our salvation in fear and trembling" (Phil 2:12).

Spatial distance naturally affects a community. Ours is a culture in which we like our personal space. When we engage in conversation with someone, it is customary to maintain several feet of space between us. We find it uncomfortable to be pressed together—be it riding the subway, sitting in a movie theatre, or sitting in a church pew. This visceral need for space is a microcosm of the psychological distance we create for ourselves when we remain aloof from community.

One way to overcome the barrier of distance that limits our communal experience is a commitment to a specific community in time and space. The Canadian artist Alex Colville, whose art has been on display at the Art Gallery of Ontario, intentionally lived for much of his life in the small university town Wolfville, Nova Scotia. He believed changing environments was a barrier to the creative process, so he chose to remain in this small town in order to paint from the perspective of truly knowing his environment. The Benedictine model of a cloistered life offers us a religious model where the monks commit to a specific monastery and live there for the duration of their lives. They do not leave the cloister to experience another place but keep going deeper to explore their own geographical space and the interiority of their psyche and souls. They understand that life's profound experiences and opportunities for growth come from penetrating one community and space.

Finally, there is the reality of experiential distance. Individuals enter a church community such as ours with disparate experiences. There is the panoply of family makeup—the two parent home, the single-parent family, the grandmother raising the children, the single person—and the difference that money brings. There are also the global issues affecting individuals who have come as refugees from war-torn situations, escaping violence and attacks on their lives. There are congregants who have lost children to street violence and others who have lost loved ones to suicide. Others come from less traumatic and more stable circumstances. How is it possible to build a healthy community within such vast experiential distance? It is only by the grace of God and serious intentionality of purpose that a community can overcome the aggregate of distances that it faces.

FROM INDIVIDUALISM TO BELONGING

Individualism and the entrepreneurial spirit have spawned significant advancements in the global village, creating immense possibilities in career paths, increased options for personal development, and exciting inventions of new products and procedures that make the world a more livable place. Many embrace the frontier spirit of striking out on one's own, carving one's own path, and following one's passions and dreams. It is an approach to life easy to applaud. However, there is an incipient danger to this individualism where we allow ego, pleasure, and personal growth to dominate. We see ourselves as self-sufficient, not really needing community. As a consequence, this independent and creative spirit can easily produce an attitude of indifference toward seeking out and entering into community. If we do enter in, we see the life of the community as a service for our consumer needs. In essence, the community is held lightly and perceived as an option. If the group serves our purposes and meets our needs, we are happy enough to continue in it. When challenges arise and we are disappointed, we extricate ourselves, moving on to another group—or none at all.

In the early church there was only one church in town and one had to persevere while remaining in a spirit of *koinōnia*. Now there are lots of churches, so why tough it out if we can have our needs met elsewhere? When community is held so precariously, we do not establish deep roots. The church is not perceived as a living organism of which we are privileged to be a part—whose vision and power is greater than our personal preferences and can powerfully speak to us. Further, when we judge the community, we put up barriers to the relationships that can potentially nurture and enrich our lives. We isolate ourselves from the group until one day we just leave. At this juncture the spirit of individualism becomes counterproductive—even destructive—weakening the essential role community plays in the health and vibrancy of our lives.

Belonging to and participating in a larger group is a deliberate choice and an extension of the initial decision to follow Christ—to become part of the body of Christ. As we commit ourselves to Jesus and his community, we develop a sense of belonging as the gathered people of God. This experience of belonging nurtures and strengthens us and can help us overcome the burnout that often comes from living in isolation. Living in community reminds us that we are gifted together and that the community has the resources to accomplish what we cannot do alone. Of course, building community takes time and cannot be rushed. Patience is required, which includes a measure of suffering. (The root of the word "patience" is the Latin *patī*, meaning "to endure," "to suffer.") We often give up on the reality of community too soon because we do not want to push through the suffering. We fear the intimacy and vulnerability required as we truly meet with one another and show our true selves. Distance and lack of transparency is much more comfortable. But this comfort is ultimately isolating and hinders our personal development.

People want a sense of belonging. They fear the process but fundamentally desire connection. Ironically, in the classroom, whether in Toronto or in Sucre, Bolivia, we observe students constantly checking their phones or tablets to see if they are being remembered. "Is anyone thinking of me right now?" It does not matter that they are already with friends. There is a prevailing anxiety of wanting more and more connection to the point of engaging in virtual community instead of with the people sitting next to them. These students are not so different from us. We all resonate with the longing for belonging, whether we recognize it as such. Henri Nouwen tells the story of moving to the L'Arche community of Daybreak as their priest in search of a greater experience of community.[8] Nouwen had taught at the prestigious Yale and Harvard Universities, but still felt isolated and burnt out. His friend Jean Vanier counseled him toward the understanding that what was lacking was true participation in community.

We may not be able to physically move into a residential community like Nouwen, but we can take steps to strengthen ties to our own spiritual communities. We need to push through the protective barriers we have erected as a way of guarding our fragile hearts. Community is not a dream state, something we imagine. It is a reality of imperfect individuals all with problems—but this is the place where we are called "to live."[9] If we persevere we will find ourselves surrounded by others who can love and accept us, returning the grace we extend.

To participate genuinely in the church community we need to be aware of what Scott Peck calls "pseudo community," where there is a superficial commitment to harmony and peace. In pseudo community, individuals avoid exploration of deeper issues for fear of stirring up group tension and disagreement. For example, churches hesitate to explore women using their spiritual gifts in ministry, or resist discussing differing baptismal practices or policies of church membership, or refuse to consider LGBTQ participation in the church. We trump the apostle Paul's exhortation for unity (Eph 4:1–6) with a commitment to our comfortable, long-held positions. In contrast, a healthy community fosters personal development and an exploration of themes that may cause tension but are necessary for the benefit of its participants. To move into this place, each member of the group needs a commitment to both honesty and respect, which will ultimately serve the greater good; authenticity and spiritual maturity become the larger goals. As personal growth takes place communal health also grows.

---

8. Nouwen, *Road to Daybreak*, 1–5, 219–28.
9. Bonhoeffer, *Life Together*, 26–30.

Part I—The Paths of Listening

HEARING GOD'S VOICE

Living in community becomes a tangible way of hearing God's voice through both the community and individuals within it.[10] As we are transparent with one another, the exchanges lead us deeper in the path of self-discovery and hearing Abba's whispers. As Calvin famously declared, borrowing from St. Augustine and Clement of Alexandra, "Without knowledge of self there is no knowledge of God; . . . without knowledge of God there is no knowledge of self."[11] As we go deeper into community we are bound to hear the voice of God through authentic human conversation. Anne Lamot, who is White, tells stories of how her incipient faith grew exponentially through participation with her young son in a small African-American church. Simple conversations with older women in the church opened spiritual windows and her relationship with God grew. She sums up the love she has for her church in these words: "And that is why I have stayed so close to mine—because no matter how bad I am feeling, how lost or lonely or frightened, when I see the faces of the people at my church, and hear their tawny voices, I can always find my way home."[12]

We assist each other in the process of hearing God's voice as we respond to one another in grace. Our own church vision statement begins with the phrase "Receiving Grace, Giving Grace," and one of the ways we try to do this is through "the ministry of listening."[13] As Bonhoeffer reminds us in his classic work *Life Together*, "the ministry of listening" speaks powerfully in the process of others coming to greater authenticity. There is no significant communication apart from listening, whether it is with others or with God. Space must be provided for the other voice to be heard, and in that hearing personal revelation and growth takes place. In listening we offer others great service as we take the time to share in their journey, and as they listen to us we also are the beneficiaries. Listening leads to friendship and sharing from both the heart and mind, as we saw illustrated in the early church community (Acts 4:32). As we embrace this alternative community it becomes a powerful witness to the love of God and his work on planet Earth.

---

10. Barry addresses these points in *Seek My Face*, 30–35.

11. Calvin, *Institutes of the Christian Religion*, vol. 1, 35, 37. See Augustine, *Confessions*, 211.

12. Lamott, *Traveling Mercies*, 55.

13. Bonhoeffer, *Life Together*, 90–108.

Finally, it is important to recognize that hearing Abba's voice is accelerated as we move towards the fragile ones. Vanier repeatedly makes this point in his writings: God is found especially in the weak, not in the rich and powerful.[14] Indeed, Jesus begins his public ministry with a similar focus, saying, "The Spirit of the Lord is upon me, because he has anointed me to bring good news to the poor. He has sent me to proclaim release to the captives and recovery of sight to the blind, to let the oppressed go free, to proclaim the year of the Lord's favor" (Luke 4:18–19). It is ironic that in church ministry we become excited if the beautiful and upwardly mobile enter our doors but hardly notice the "little ones" who come faithfully week after week. In my experience, it is consistently the "weak ones" who make the greatest contribution to the experience of *koinōnia*. The fragile ones—the children, the elderly, the persons with physical or intellectual challenges—become the glue that holds the community together. As the community serves these people it remains healthy and strong. As we forget the little ones we become lost in power games and internal strife and lose our capacity to hear the subtle murmurs of Abba in the midst of the external noise. In my own faith community, I lead a small Bible study every other week made up of retired Jamaican women, a few Caucasian retirees, a high school teacher, and a middle-aged man who suffered a head injury from a motorcycle accident. The group does not represent the power shakers of the world. Some might say my commitment in time is poorly placed and it would be more strategic to interact with people of influence. I disagree. These folk represent the majority of the church who live faithfully in a challenging neighborhood. The Bible study we do is a simple reading and discussion of the text, supporting the individuals in their devotion to know and follow Jesus. Regular interaction through the week sustains them as they face trials. As Bonhoeffer suggests, "The Christ in his own heart is weaker than the Christ in the word of his brother/sister; his own heart is uncertain, his brother's is sure."[15] A life together in community allows the Spirit of God to freely flow through its parts, bringing fresh resources to each member (1 Cor 12). Our encouragement is to actively participate in such a community and to pay attention to it and the voices of its members as a means of hearing Abba's voice.

---

14. Vanier, *Broken Body*, 1–3.
15. Bonhoeffer, *Life Together*, 23.

Part I—The Paths of Listening

QUESTIONS FOR REFLECTION

1. Most of us struggle at some level with enthusiastically participating in community. What are the hindrances that keep you from engaging in community life?

2. A sense of belonging is a key dimension of remaining in community. What factors promote your appreciation of the group and your awareness of belonging to it?

3. In your experience how have you heard from Abba either through the group or individual members?

4. In your journal keep track of how you are hearing the whispers of Abba through community life. Especially pay attention to the specific ways that God has spoken to you in the past and where he may now be speaking into your life.

Chapter 7

Celebration
The Song of the Heart

AFTER A DOZEN YEARS at my first church, I spent a year working in a group home with an organization committed to caring for the needs of individuals with physical and intellectual challenges. It was a demanding year in many ways—a total change in direction in a physically strenuous environment that required new skills and shift work for less money. At the same time it was a year of considerable joy as I came to appreciate the core individuals and their gift of immediate presence in living each day. When they were happy they were ecstatic! When they were grumpy they were miserable! Celebrations like birthdays and Christmas were especially exciting. The residents would cry with joy when receiving a gift, eating a good meal, decorating the Christmas tree, or going on an outing to the mall; these individuals knew how to celebrate with laughter, jokes, clapping, songs, and dance. They certainly taught us as counselors how to be present and real in the moment, if we were willing to pay attention and be receptive to their gifts. My specific charge was a young man named Mike. He was a reflective individual of few words but when he smiled he lit up the entire room. In spite of the emotional pain he carried from years of institutional living, he taught me how to be still, how to smile, how to enjoy food, and how to persevere through trials.

The Scriptures also teach us about understanding celebration and the act of celebrating. The Old Testament festivals of Passover, Pentecost, and

Part I—The Paths of Listening

Sukkot (Tabernacles or Booths) were weeklong celebrations of God's work and presence in the life of the nation. Passover celebrated God's redeeming work of bringing Israel out of bondage and became an annual remembrance of God's saving power and liberation (Exod 13; Deut 16:1–8). Pentecost was originally a harvest festival giving thanks for God's provision (Lev 23:9–21; Deut 16:9–10), but over time became associated with the giving of the Torah as a gift and guide for living.[1] Sukkot was the highpoint of celebration in Israel's cycle of festivals. It celebrated God's providential care throughout Israel's wilderness wanderings and became known as a festival of joy, as people lived in *sukkahs* (booths) throughout the week, exchanging stories of God's care with family and friends and rejoicing in God's abundance with food and drink (Lev 23:34, 39).[2] The book of Nehemiah records an actual celebration of Sukkot during the postexilic epoch, and rings with the words, "The joy of the Lord is your strength" (8:10). Strassfeld provides a description of a *sukkah* constructed during the festival:

> It is open to the heavens, open to God's sheltering presence. It is under the wings of the Shekhinah (God) that we can find real security, real shelter, not in our homes, no matter how strong or elaborate they are. Skhakh [ie., sukka] is simultaneously a sign of our vulnerability to the vicissitudes of the world and also of the reassuring shelter of the Holy One who once led a people into the desert and out again.[3]

During the season of Sukkot we are not to be sad. Instead, we are invited to focus on Abba's presence and his ongoing provision while living in dependence under his caring hand. The annunciation of Sukkot—"Don't give up on God! Rejoice! Trust, for the world rests in his sheltering arms!"—needs to continually ring in our ears as we dwell in a society prone to despair and fatalism.

The Scriptures also affirm that the ministry of Jesus began and ended with a call to joy. Richard Foster comments,

> Celebration is at the heart of the way of Christ. He entered the world on a high note of jubilation: 'I bring you good news of a great joy,' cried the angel, 'which shall come to all people' (Luke 2:10). He left the world bequeathing His joy to the disciples: 'These

---

1. Strassfeld, *Jewish Holidays*, 69.
2. See Ibid., 139, on *sukkah* activities.
3. Ibid., 143.

things I have spoken to you that my joy may be in you, and that your joy may be full' (John 15:11)."[4]

Throughout his ministry Jesus attended weddings, supplied the needs of a host and hostess by turning water into wine when their wine ran out (saving them considerable embarrassment) (John 2:1–11), and received and blessed little ones in spite of his disciples' criticism (Matt 19:13–15). He also attended parties, banquets, and other festivities, to the point of being labeled a wine bibber and a free spirit (Luke 7:33–35). Jesus determined to enjoy community of all sorts and was not hesitant to celebrate the special occasions of life. We are sure he celebrated the birthdays of all twelve disciples on their own special days. I would also wager that Jesus had an amazing smile—just like my charge, Mike—a smile that lifted the spirits of both sinners and saints, rich and poor, Jews and Gentiles, men and women alike.

THE TENDENCY TO RESIST CELEBRATION

The Scriptures, on the other hand, also reveal a hesitancy to celebrate on a variety of occasions. Jonah was enjoined to preach the good news to the Ninevites but he refused by fleeing to the end of the world, then known as Tarshish. Later, he prepared a shelter from the sun and proceeded to sit in rage waiting to see if God might change his mind and destroy the city after all (Jonah 1:1–3; 4:5). Michal critiqued her husband David as he danced before the Lord, and she refused to enter into a spirit of celebration even after he had led the troops and defeated the Philistines (2 Sam 6:16–23). Stephen had a vision of the resurrected Christ standing at the right hand of God and the authorities of the day rejected his vision and stoned him to death (Acts 7:56–60). Peter was invited by the Lord to join in a festive meal but declined to eat what God had made clean (Acts 10:9–16). Indeed, God made the request three different times and Peter obstinately refused on each occasion.

Just like these biblical characters, our own habits and prejudices often shut down opportunities for celebration. We either do not want to hear from God or our own learned behavior patterns are too deeply entrenched and we miss the invitation to join the party. On one hand, we are simply children of a cynical and blasé age. We are so accustomed to extreme visuals, sounds, and spectacles that it takes an ever-increasing flood of sensations to

---

4. Foster, *Celebration of Discipline*, 163.

make an impact on us. The sound has to be bigger, the special effects more extreme. As Jean Vanier observes, "In richer countries we have lost the art of celebrating. People go to movies or watch television or have other leisure activities; they go to parties, but they do not celebrate."[5]

Spiritual writers attach different names to our resistance to celebration. Kathleen Norris writes about the malaise of *acedia*, a condition hard to pin down, which has gripped our Western society. Indeed, this "absence of care" is nothing new, she points out:

> Evagrius marked acedia as one of the spiritual afflictions, far more deadly than the more physical temptations such as gluttony or lust, or the melancholy arising from deprivation or anger. Acedia, he insisted, is something more, a weariness of soul . . . which in the early monastic world was always linked with prayer.[6]

One of the results of the power of *acedia* is the rejection of "place," which takes many forms—the leaving of a faith community, a job, a marriage. *Acedia* tells us it is nobler to walk away and find self-fulfillment than remain rooted to one place.[7] As a pastor I see the negative imprint of *acedia* regularly. Individuals claim that their needs are not being met in the community and that change is required for spiritual growth. More often than not *acedia* has reared its head and change for change's sake is the true motivation for the departure. And the cycle repeats itself, where the new and exciting quickly becomes the old and routine. But if we keep constantly on the move, we limit the potential power of community and its positive role in our lives.

Linked with both cynicism and *acedia* is a powerful counterpart—apathy. Apathy similarly limits our ability to celebrate because we just do not want to expend the energy required. Celebration feels too laborious. It is easier to watch life go by and remain in the role of spectator. Roberta Bondi addresses the power of apathy in our day where we focus on our own needs and shut out anything else that seems foreign to our immediate concerns. She suggests a subtle form of apathy is demonstrated in a generally warm enthusiasm for humanity but a resistance to specific compassion. She explains, "It is very easy to love in the abstract—the homeless, children, suffering. It is not

---

5. Vanier, *Community and Growth*, 313.
6. Norris, *Acedia and Me*, 25.
7. Ibid., 25.

so hard to love those with whom we have infrequent or only surface contact when love is defined as a kind of unfocused friendly feeling."[8]

Akin to apathy is the modern attitude of boredom. Margaret Vissers defines it as "a feeling of fury reacting to repetitiveness, or alternatively a sense of emptiness, of finding nothing worth doing, let alone striving for; it is the experience of dullness and generalized meaninglessness."[9] These are strong words, impressing on us the seriousness of this condition. Furthermore, she connects boredom with the rise of consumerism:

> Boredom is the motivating force of a consumer society. Bored people buy stuff for temporary relief from their condition. Feeling flat? Let me offer you a car, a pair of shoes, a cruise. Distract yourself: you'll forget about your boredom for a while—until obligingly, you require relief once more. Boredom is not only a result but a 'sine qua non' of consumerism."[10]

Boredom attaches itself to apathy, isolating us from any concerns for our neighbors. It forces us toward ego and away from participation in community and celebration. The individual may still have an urge to party but it is based on a need for stimulus and sensation as opposed to an authentic desire to celebrate life with others.

Finally, we resist celebration due to an internal fear that we do not either merit the reward or are afraid we will lose the moments of celebration we do receive. We live with the nagging fear that if people discover who we really are our success will be taken away. "I am not worthy to engage in celebration." "If I start celebrating I will lose everything because people will perceive the sham of my life." This self-talk is not logical, but based on apprehensions that we carry concerning our self-worth. A sense of doom or fate covers our lives, casting a shadow of doubt; it is only a matter of time before things fall apart. Celebrating would simply hasten the pending collapse.

MOVING TOWARDS CELEBRATION

These celebration resistors contrast greatly with the attitudes I experienced at a birthday party for a friend's seven-year-old in the city of Cochabamba. As is the custom in many Spanish cultures, the party for Paulo ended with

---

8. Bondi, *To Pray and to Love*, 32.
9. Visser, *Beyond Fate*, 141.
10. Ibid., 141.

the breaking of the piñata. The children took turns hitting the piñata until it split open and out tumbled candies, toys, balloons, and noisemakers. When the items fell to the ground the young children started to gather up the loot—except for Daniel, a child standing on the outer circle of the group crying. For some reason he was not participating; he just watched and cried. What happened next was beautiful. The rest of the children gathered around, consoling him and sharing from their treasures, drawing him into the celebration. Without the prodding of adults, the children on their own accord included their young friend in the celebration. As I admired the children's instinctive kindness, I also wondered how much of our refusal to celebrate is similar to that little boy's holding back, stopped by our own pain and self-consciousness. Daniel needed the loving actions of the rest of the group to enter into the party. Perhaps we also can learn to celebrate and be drawn into a spirit of celebration as Daniel's friends demonstrated.

What helps us overcome the shadow side that hinders our movement towards celebration? We begin by reaffirming the connection between celebration and our experience of community. Celebration flows from a sense of living within a vital community. It is limited when we live in isolation and feel that everything depends on our own actions. Jean Vanier, a key proponent of celebration, reminds us that it is "a communal experience of joy, a song of thanksgiving. We celebrate the fact of being together." He goes on to describe how we have lost this communal sense, and hence do not know how to celebrate:

> [R]ich societies have lost their sense of tradition and so their sense of celebration as well. Celebration is linked to family and religious tradition. As soon as it gets away from this, it tends to become artificial, and people need stimulants like alcohol to get it moving. Then it is no longer a celebration.[11]

So the first step in recovering a sense of celebration is regaining an experience of community. Instead of moving away from community we need to move towards it. As Vanier encourages us, we need to re-establish the communal connection. There is a need to balance our desire for individualism with a healthy respect and valuing of communal life and the benefits that flow from it. This desire leads toward reconnecting with the faith community.

---

11. Vanier, *Community and Growth*, 313.

Celebration

Another specific step we can take is reclaiming the importance of hospitality. The Greek word *philoxenia*, translated as "love of the stranger" in the New Testament, has to do with reaching out to the "other" and not merely one's friends (1 Tim 3:2; Titus 1:8). Jesus illustrates the reality of hospitality in his powerful parable of the sheep and the goats (Matt 25:31–46), teaching that as people minister to the poor and hurting "you do it to me" (v. 40). The authors of *Slow Church* see Jesus' words as "a stunning picture of the upside-down kingdom. The world is God's and everything in it. We live by divine hospitality. And yet we are given the opportunity—even the command—to offer hospitality to God by caring for the people who are the most vulnerable."[12] In this act of moving closer to people (especially those who are marginalized in any way) there is the opportunity to learn and share new things that can lead us to celebration. As we demonstrate a welcoming spirit, individuals are encouraged to relax and trust in the exchange of each other's lives. Through this interchange we are able to recognize God's presence and his image in the other person, leading us to deeper relationships, gratitude, and opportunities for joy. Further, the times of hospitality provide rich soil for the spontaneous eruption of new words from Abba that percolate at subterranean depths, waiting for an opening in the fissures of our lives.

Intertwined with hospitality is the act of eating together and the conversations that emerge from such encounters. Smith and Pattison point out that "sharing a meal with someone is one of the most intimate things we can do."[13] That intimacy is heightened and strengthened as we take another step towards regaining a spirit of celebration. When we share a meal together and engage in conversation we experience the dynamics of Sukkot.[14] We speak gratefully of God's goodness in terms of how he provides, cares, and shepherds his children. The interchange between family members leads to celebration as different generations enter the conversation and each one hears the voices of family, friends, and visitors. Of course, this type of meal takes time and energy and is a contrast to the modern hurried meal we often experience. As we slow down and share a meal together and take the time for real conversation, moments of true joy and insight are bound to happen as we allow for the creative spark to pass from person to person around the table. Eating together and conversation work as vital ingredients

---

12. Smith and Pattison, *Slow Church*, 198.
13. Ibid., 201.
14. Ibid. See ch. 11, "Dinner Table Conversation as a Way of Being Church," 208–22.

of hospitality, nurturing individuals, families, and faith communities, and ultimately impact the broader community by instilling a spirit of sharing for the stranger in our midst.

To this end it is important to recognize that hospitality, shared meals, and movement towards celebration require a degree of planning. There is a need to prime the pump for celebration to freely flow. It is unrealistic to expect individuals in our joyless society to spontaneously enter into it. Jean Vanier makes this point from his observation in the L'Arche communities: "We have a duty to learn more creative ways of celebrating. We need to find more rousing and funnier songs, stories, and snippets of information." He insightfully adds, "A celebration or other community activity should be at least as carefully prepared as a meal. Things cannot be left to happen spontaneously.[15]

It is unfortunate that church gatherings often lack this level of planning. We act as if there is nothing we can do to draw people together other than to provide a possible forum for connection. We organize the menu, seating, decorations, and even invite special talent to perform, but we do not take specific steps to help people make connections. Such a position is insufficient for creating a healthy environment for celebration and joy. Conversely, there is great benefit in designing and implementing activities that draw individuals into conversation and providing them paths for overcoming a reticence to participate.

LISTENING AND CELEBRATION

The heart of celebration flows from the practice of gratitude and thankfulness, and the key word is "practice." As we have observed, the forces of anti-celebration are numerous and powerful. We only overcome these negative voices through a concerted effort to pay attention to the blessings and good gifts that Abba provides. As James reminds us, "Every generous act of giving, with every perfect gift, is from above, coming down from the Father of lights, with whom there is no variation or shadow due to change" (Jas 1:17). There is great import in being aware of God's daily provision and shepherding. When we start to take the richness of life for granted we miss the daily miracles that constantly rain down. He invites us to pay attention and give him concrete praise for the abundance of each day—for today's health, today's provision, today's joy, today's peace! As we develop

---

15. Vanier, *Community and Growth*, 324, 325.

this practice of gratitude we begin to wake up to life's daily blessings. Everything is gift: birth, human development, intellectual and creative talents; we simply receive and nurture what has been given. There is no room for pride—only space for thanks! Our responsibility is to develop the practice of gratitude like any other discipline, such as playing the guitar, speaking a second language, or playing a sport.

My travels in Latin America have funded my appreciation of how thankfulness leads to a spirit of celebration. I have witnessed more than one Bolivian faith community seize the moment of their church anniversary and get the whole congregation involved in the process. Their festivities include bands, parades, costumes, dancing, special *tortas* (cakes), meals, storytelling—and all of this over an entire week of special activities. And these churches embark on this kind of celebration yearly. The anniversary is seen as an opportunity to celebrate and to have a party including every person in the community. The Bolivians enter into this kind of celebration with passion and joy as they seek to remember God's work in their midst. Their spirit of gratitude is reminiscent of Israel's rejoicing in the festival of Sukkot. Such a commitment to celebrate a church anniversary contrasts significantly with the perfunctory effort that commonly happens here in the North—even in our own church community! We are so slow to embrace the celebratory spirit of the meek Bolivian church with its meager riches. How is it that they are so determined to party?

As we celebrate, we place ourselves in an environment where it is easier to discern the voice of God in our lives. We think of Zacchaeus. When Jesus invites himself to lunch, the tax collector is impressed with the celebratory spirit of Jesus and his disciples to the point where he makes amends with all those he has swindled. He hears something new from Abba (Luke 19:1–10). Then there are Cleopas and his friend with Jesus on the road to Emmaus and their recognition of him during the meal (Luke 24:13–35). Eating together uncovers their relationship and leads them from mourning his death to a celebration of his resurrection and a return to the community in Jerusalem. Celebration opens the eyes of one's heart and unplugs the blocked ears that have become dull to the Spirit. As we move away from the margins and towards the center, the Spirit moves us into places where we hear new whispers from Abba. May we keep listening, open our hands, and come to his banqueting party.

Part I—The Paths of Listening

QUESTIONS FOR FURTHER REFLECTION

1. Sukkot is a festival of joy for the Jewish community that is celebrated year after year. Are there annual events in your calendar that provide opportunities for joy and celebration? Name them and write them down in your journal. Reflect upon these occasions and consider how you can maximize the celebration theme for you and your family.

2. We resist celebrating for a variety of reasons. What are the hurdles that exist that hinder your from entering into a spirit of celebration? Share with a friend (perhaps a member of a small group) how you might deal with these barriers.

3. Hospitality and dinner table conversations are ways forward in embracing an attitude of celebration. Start sketching out steps you can take to open your home to others for meals and conversations. Who might you invite for such times? Are there people from your church who would appreciate an offer of hospitality? Consider inviting individuals who are not part of your immediate circle of friends. Maybe you will make a friend and learn something new about life.

4. Celebration becomes fertile ground for hearing the voice of Abba. Has there been a connection between celebrating and hearing from God in your life? If so then write down some story and share it with a friend. If your friend also has a story then listen and celebrate with him or her. Mutual storytelling often reveals insights to both speaker and listener. Enter in and see what happens.

PART II

The Practice of Listening

Chapter 8

An Invitation to Pay Attention

ABBA'S OVERTURES ARE SUBTLE by nature and come to us, more often than not, as whispers and not clarion calls. Our wordy world masks the quiet, respectful voice of God with the incessant noise of a plugged-in culture. In light of this sensorial overload it is helpful to explore, as we have done here, the different paths that can lead us out of the barrage of competing voices: the act of praise, the sacrament of creation, silence and solitude, the Word, prayer, our life together, and intentional celebration. Each of these avenues takes us to that place where we can hear Abba's voice and experience the constant imprint of the Holy Spirit upon our lives.

At the same time, we need to embrace practices that will strengthen our desire for God and enable us to recognize his whispers. Not unlike Brother Lawrence of centuries ago, we need to "practice the presence of God" as we retrain ourselves to be receptors of Abba's overtures. We must exchange old patterns of living with new ways of seeing and hearing. Accessing Abba's communication is like receiving the clear signal of a radio station in our car. As we fine-tune the signal, we will hear Abba's whisper with greater clarity, certainty, and power.

In C. S. Lewis's *The Silver Chair*, Aslan sends Jill on a mission to join her friend Eustace in helping rescue a captured prince. Before he blows her into Narnia, Aslan gives Jill four instructions with accompanying signs to remember—a task harder than she anticipates. He emphasizes the importance of staying alert:

PART II—THE PRACTICE OF LISTENING

> But, first, remember, remember, remember the signs.... And whatever strange things may happen to you, let nothing turn your mind from following the signs. And secondly, I give you a warning. Here on the mountain I have spoken to you clearly; I will not often do so down in Narnia. Here on the mountain, the air is clear and your mind is clear; as you drop down into Narnia, the air will thicken. Take great care that it does not confuse your mind. And the signs which you have learned here will not look at all as you expect them to look, when you meet them there. That is why it is so important to know them by heart and pay no attention to appearances. Remember the signs and believe the signs. Nothing else matters.[1]

It is a spiritual lesson Aslan gives to Jill—one applicable to all travelers on life's journey. When we are in our own world—our Narnia, so to speak—"the air will thicken" and it can confuse our minds. We need to be alert and disciplined, paying attention to "signs," the whispers of Abba.

The apostle Paul speaks with the same urgency to the Ephesian Christians and to his young colleagues Timothy and Titus. In his writings we hear the repeated refrain to "pay attention," "wake up," "consider," "be devoted to"—all calling his readers to be aware of their experience in the moment. In Ephesians 5 he strings together a series of admonitions: "Sleeper, awake! Rise from the dead, and Christ will shine on you" (v. 14); "Be careful then how you live" (v. 15); "making the most of your time" (v. 16); "do not be foolish, but understand what the will of the Lord is" (v. 17); "giving thanks to God the Father at all times" (v. 20). Paul prefaces the unit with the exhortation "to live not as unwise but as wise" people. He encourages us to be reflective in living our lives and addressing our choices, our time, and what we pay attention to. Do we live in excess and lose our self-control (v. 18) or do we live thoughtfully and give thanks to God (vv. 19–20)? Do we seek simply to satisfy our own desires or do we open ourselves up to the filling and working of the Holy Spirit in our lives for the benefit of others (v.v 18–20)?

In the pastoral epistles Paul mentors his young assistants, calling them to "pay attention" to how they are filling up their lives and what voices they are following. "Train yourself in godliness," he tells Timothy (1 Tim 4:7); "Pay close attention to yourself and to your teaching" (1 Tim 4:16); "pursue righteousness, godliness, faith, love, endurance, gentleness. Fight the good fight of faith; take hold of the eternal life, to which you were called" (1 Tim 6:11–12). He advises Titus to be very careful in his teaching so that the sound gospel

---

1. Lewis, *Silver Chair*, 25–26.

An Invitation to Pay Attention

is proclaimed, the ethical life is followed and the new church is established: "Put in order what remained to be done" (Titus 1:5); "teach what is consistent with sound doctrine" (2:1); "insist on these things, so that those who have come to believe in God may be careful to devote themselves to good works" (3:8). In all these instructions Paul adjures the churches that he shepherds to examine their living patterns. In their call we hear our own invitation to pay attention—to not drift aimlessly. Paul uses a variety of words for "pay attention": *tereō* (watch or observe; 1 Tim 6:14), *agrypneō* (be awake, keep watch; Eph 6:18), *gymnazō* (train, exercise; 1 Tim 4:7), and *epēkō* (aim at, take pains; 1 Tim 4:16); however, they all share the sense of being thoughtful, reflective, and careful in how one lives life. It is the opposite of drifting or reacting to stimuli. It is a call to wake up, have insight, "see into" what is happening in the steps and choices of each day.

One of the significant challenges in paying attention is the hurdle of distraction. Distraction literally means "to be pulled apart" or "to be divided." In this state we often feel anxious and nervous about past actions or future possibilities. We experience a low-level anxiety that makes it difficult to stay present and aware of our immediate surroundings. Distraction is endemic to our culture. We use smartphones while walking; we text while driving; we listen to music with earphones while running. These common actions distance us from our immediate settings and limit attention to our present reality. We all face this challenge of distraction, whether in our work, parenting, relationships, or in the setting and achievement of goals. Just as Aslan warns Jill in *The Silver Chair*, our air is thick with competing thoughts and obligations, diversions, and distraction. How do we learn the skill of paying attention?

COMING TO AWARENESS

To begin, we need *to want* to pay attention. It is a choice to become alert to our surroundings, as Margaret Visser suggests in her 2002 CBC Massey Lectures, *Beyond Fate*.[2] As the title of her lectures and book suggest, she is speaking to a culture—our culture—that is unwittingly trapped by a kind

---

2. Visser, *Beyond Fate*, 143–44. She herself explains that she is drawing on Bernard Lonergan's Transcendental Precepts—"stages and levels on a journey upwards and out of flat fatalism: Be attentive; Be intelligent; Be reasonable . . . ; Be responsible." Lonergan, a longstanding professor at Regis College, University of Toronto, is considered to be one of the leading thinkers of the twentieth century both as a theologian and philosopher.

of fatalism. The key to her argument is choice—desire and will. Then action follows as we choose to engage. She outlines four steps to this kind of awareness: (1) pay attention, (2) concentrate, (3) question, and (4) respond to one's awareness. What she suggests is applicable to our pursuit and practice of hearing Abba's whispers.

First, as she reminds her listeners, it is a discipline to become aware of our surroundings. It is a choice not to float through life in a distracted state but to truly experience the day as it unfolds—"to be disinterested—that is, to be interested in things in and for themselves, and not because of possible profits for yourself—and especially to pay attention to what is supposed to be boring or taken for granted."[3] Jesus demonstrated this capacity to appreciate the details of his day, whether in observing nature or responding to individuals through the day. He encouraged his listeners to be aware of the birds, the flowers, the animals, the seasons (Matt 6:25–34; 7:15–20)—daily sights that we often ignore in our busy schedules. Jesus also demonstrated the capacity to live "in the passive voice," as Thomas Kelly encourages.[4] "Living in the passive voice" refers to a willingness to respond to individuals spontaneously, as seen in the request of the woman with the hemorrhage who sought healing (Matt 10:20), or Jairus asking Jesus to come and heal his dying daughter (Mark 5:23). Jesus was willing to change his schedule as he became aware of other people's needs. Sadly, we often experience tunnel vision as we focus on our own agendas and are unaware of the legitimate concerns of others that arise in our day. With awareness we create sufficient space to experience our days, moment by moment. We deliberately slow the pace and do not hurry from one thing to another so that details can be seen.

The world of diving offers its own object lesson: I travelled to the Philippines with my friend Rob to explore the rich underwater world of the South Pacific in the famous coral triangle bordering Indonesia, Malaysia, the Philippines, and Papua New Guinea. The area is replete with diverse corals such as finger, elkhorn, fire, and table corals, and an abundant variety of colorful fish life, including schools of angels, triggers, barracudas, rays, and green turtles. However, to our surprise, this time we experienced a new form of diving rich in biodiversity called "muck diving," in which one literally dives close to the mucky, flat bottom of the sea, peering for minute sea life. This style of diving requires one to slow down to a crawl and look closely to see the tiny sea horses, spiders, crabs, and fish. If one travels

---

3. Ibid., 143.
4. Kelly, *Testament of Devotion*, 34.

quickly, absolutely nothing is seen except expanses of grey mud! One has to travel slowly, quietly, and with attentive eyes to enjoy the richness of this corner of God's creation.

In the film *Still Alice*, a middle-aged professor at Columbia University is diagnosed with early Alzheimer's disease and experiences a rapid decline in her memory and coping skills. In a poignant scene Alice is out jogging through her university campus when she has the terrified realization that she is completely lost. Her increasing incapacities go on to play havoc with her relationship with her husband and three adult children as they all try to cope with the new reality of their family life. In another powerful vignette Alice painstakingly prepares and delivers a lecture for a meeting of the Alzheimer's Society, where she describes the decline of losing her life and mind as "hell." Yet Alice describes how she still has moments in the day of happiness and joy: "I am not suffering. I am struggling to be part of this journey—to stay connected to who I once was. I live in the moment. It is all I can do. I live in the moment." We are all similarly invited to open our eyes and live with awareness in the moment. The present moment is all we ever have. We do not have the past and we never experience the future. Alice painfully acknowledges that "the competitive, achieving Alice" is gone, and embracing "the Alice in the moment" is where her joy is found. A great deal of joy awaits us if we, too, are able to embrace the moment and learn to develop the ability of living with awareness.

CONCENTRATION AND QUESTIONING

Waking up to awareness leads us to Visser's second step: concentration. As we encounter new things (like strange little creatures in muck diving), we are invited to focus on what we see and attempt to understand what we are observing. Concentration involves the use of our intelligence through reflection and by making connections with other related entities and data.[5] For example, on another dive excursion in the South Pacific, my friend and I came across large patches of finger anemones. Amidst the anemones, small orange, white, yellow, and black clown fish make their home. The anemones are dangerous to other fish, but are safe for these small fish, which have developed immunity to their stinging tentacles. A beautiful synergy is achieved as the little clown fish dance in and out of the jelly-like fingers. The clown fish pop out to catch food and then return quickly to the safety of home base, hiding

---

5. See Lonergan, *Method in Theology*, 15–16, 20.

from larger predators in the safety of the tentacles. For their part, the clown fish protect home turf by quickly shooting out and nipping intruders like the butterfly fish, who want to eat the tentacles—something I experienced firsthand, as a courageous clown fish bit my index finger in a moment of exploration. Through paying attention I came into awareness of the anemone patch growing on the side of the coral wall and began to understand the symbiosis between anemone and clown fish.

It is this connection between attention, awareness, and concentration that the apostle Paul is encouraging in his words to Timothy and Titus. When Paul says to Timothy, "Pay close attention to yourself" (1 Tim 4:16) or "train yourself in godliness" (4:7), he is encouraging him to reflect on his behavior and relationships and evaluate if they are helpful and pleasing to both God and the community. With concentration we try to understand what we are seeing and the implications of it in the wider scope of our field of vision. Anthony de Mello tells the story of a journalist who seeks out a guru to determine if he is the genuine thing. The wise man concurs that he is indeed a guru because he has the ability to see "the butterfly in a caterpillar, the eagle in an egg, the saint in a selfish person."[6] As we come into awareness and concentrate on what we are seeing we come into "insight"—that is, we see into the reality of what is and appreciate the beauty of what exists.

Visser presents the third step of paying attention as the practice of questioning what we see.[7] She is referring to the need to constantly check and question what we determine to be true, so that we do not become stuck in lethargic thinking patterns that have lost their energy and fruitfulness. The fear of change and disappointing people's expectations can keep us mired in articulated positions we no longer dynamically hold. Continually asking questions keeps the dialogue vibrant and we avoid becoming spiritually stuck. Jesus constantly posed questions to friends and foes alike to lead them in their spiritual exploration. He asked the sick man at the pool of Beth-zatha, "Do you want to be made well?" (John 5:6). "Are you ready to embrace a healthy life?," he asked the father of the sick boy. "Do you have faith that I am able to heal your son?" evokes the honest reply, "I believe; help my unbelief!" (Mark 9:24). When people were turning away because of his puzzling words "eat my flesh and drink my blood," he asked his nervous disciples, "Do you also wish to go away?" (John 6:67); he invited them

---

6. De Mello, *One Minute Wisdom*, 206.
7. Visser, *Beyond Fate*, 143.

to seek a deeper relationship with himself rather than simply enjoying his celebrity status. On the road to Emmaus Jesus joined the conversation of two discouraged disciples, asking, "What are you discussing?" (Luke 24:17) in order to help them process their pain and guide them into hope.

The asking of questions leads us farther along the path of paying attention. Questions cause us to consider our perspective from different angles, providing a fuller picture and sharpening our awareness of what we see. Sometimes individuals shy away from asking hard questions as they worry about what might happen to their faith. The reticence is understandable, but it is important for us to keep thinking and probing concerning our relationship with God. Paul frequently encourages us "to renovate our minds" (Col 3:2), and this happens as we concentrate and ask healthy questions, not giving into fear, but trusting that the Spirit will lead us further into the light of his truth.

RESPONDING AND LOVING

Visser's fourth step in the process of paying attention is "giving a response" or "being responsible," as Lonergan describes in his Transcendental Precepts.[8] We become aware, we concentrate, we question, and then we assume responsibility for the action we take. We see this dynamic at play in the story of Jesus at the home of Martha and Mary when Martha is complaining to Jesus that her sister is not helping to prepare the meal. Meanwhile, Mary sits at Jesus' feet, listening to his words. Mary has evaluated the situation and made the decision that paying attention to Jesus is more important than pleasing her sister and fixing the meal. It seems that Jesus concurs with Mary, as he says, "Martha, Martha, you are worried and distracted by many things. There is need of only one thing. Mary has chosen the better part, which will not be taken from her" (Luke 10:41–42). It is important to recognize that we all make choices in freedom; we all are responsible for our actions. We cannot cast blame on anyone else as we act on our own choices. However, we can trust that as we have carefully considered the various possibilities, we will choose the fruitful option flowing from an attentive and aware mind.

Lonergan adds a fifth precept, which he calls "the dynamic state of being in love," referring to the love of God, humanity, and all of nature.[9] He

8. Visser, *Beyond Fate*, 144. See also Lonergan, *Method in Theology*, 20.

9. Lonergan, *Method in Theology*, 115. For an expansion of Lonergan's understanding

asserts that for an action to be responsible it must move us personally and as a broader community towards love. If we fall short of this, we act selfishly and this is a movement away from love. We readily see this movement in the self-indulgent actions of greed, seeking power over others, hate, apathy, prejudice, and neglect of those in need. When we act for our own wellbeing at the expense of others, the ego is dominant and the community suffers. We observe the same pattern of choosing self over love on a national basis as we enjoy clean and plentiful water, clean air, low food prices, and abundant energy resources at the expense of other nations that have limited access to the same benefits. Consequently, there is a moral imperative to fund our decisions in love rather than in greed, pleasure, comfort, or our standard of living. The question then becomes, what enables the path of love? We suggest two movements that lead us in this direction both personally and communally.

LOVE: THE PRACTICE OF GRATITUDE

The first movement is the practice of gratitude. Many writers of spiritual formation talk about the significance of gratitude. Thomas Merton writes, "Gratitude therefore takes nothing for granted, is never unresponsive, is constantly awakening to new wonder and to praise of the goodness of God."[10] Don Postema suggests, "Gratitude as recognition, receptivity, and response is a basic attitude and action of the Christian life."[11] These writers undoubtedly draw on the apostle Paul in his admonitions to have hearts of thankfulness: "Do not worry about anything, but in everything by prayer and supplication with thanksgiving let your requests be made known to God" (Phil 4:6); "Devote yourselves to prayer, keeping alert in it with thanksgiving" (Col 4:2); "Give thanks in all circumstances; for this is the will of God in Christ Jesus for you" (1 Thess 5:18). Gratitude makes real and objective differences in how we live and experience our lives.

Two friends of ours established an online gratitude bulletin called "The Gratitude Workout" for a consulting project. For its duration individuals were asked to record an observation of gratitude once a day for thirty days. Here is a response that came out of the month-long exercise:

---

of love see also 115–16, 242–43.

10. Merton, *Thoughts in Solitude*, 43.
11. Postema, *Space for God*, 76.

"I didn't realize how much this workout had affected me until this morning. Over the weekend I took time to think of how I was going to respond without coming to many meaningful conclusions. Last night something happened . . . it was raining and the basement of our brand new house started filling up. My husband and I were forced to move many things including 300–400 pounds of sheet rock. I lost hold of it and it fell on me, pinning and cutting me, producing bruising and swelling. I went to bed but found it difficult to sleep. What struck me as I reflected on the experience was that I didn't, as usual, play out in my head who was going to get phone calls this morning about the mishap, but instead began running through who and what I was grateful for—from the beginning my parents, their advice and love, my family/home/work—all the way through to being grateful for just cuts, bruises and swelling. When I slept—I slept peacefully—when I woke up I was amazed at how this gratitude workout had changed my outlook! Thank you!" Cindy.

Nurturing gratitude changes our perception of the world, where, like Cindy, we can transform our perception and see "negative" happenings from a completely different perspective. We move from self-centeredness to a position of valuing others, life, and God. We appreciate the graces that consistently pour out upon us. This spirit of thanks opens up a receptivity to love and encourages our own practice of charity towards others both near and far.

LOVE: THE SPIRITUAL SENSES

A second movement is suggested by the psalmist's words, "O taste and see that the Lord is good" (Ps 34:8). The psalmist encourages us to directly experience the person of God and not to settle for a distant relationship with him. Indeed, we experience Abba before we understand his working in our lives. If we observe a one-year-old child, we see that taste and touch are her primary ways for exploring and understanding her surroundings; the senses of sight, smell, and sound follow the immediacy of taste and touch. At our grandson's first birthday he received a set of colored and patterned plastic balls. It was fascinating to watch him "taste and see" in his exploration as he held and felt the different indented patterns, putting them to his mouth and exploring them with his lips and tongue.

Part II—The Practice of Listening

In a similar way the spiritual senses parallel our physical senses. In the Gospels we read of John laying his head on the bosom of Christ; this intimate action of touch reveals his desire to be emotionally and spiritually close with his Lord. The Song of Solomon describes the desire to know the lover through the sense of smell: "Your anointing oils are fragrant, your name is perfume poured out; therefore the maidens love you. Draw me after you, let us make haste" (1:3–4). For the writer, the sense of smell portrays a passion to experience God even as a fragrance conjures up memories of the beloved's presence. The sense of taste further portrays intimacy in the bond of mother and child, as revealed in the psalmist's words, "I have calmed and quieted my soul, like a weaned child with its mother; my soul is like the weaned child that is with me" (Ps 131:2). Thomas Keating describes the impact of spiritual taste:

> It is one thing to be so close as to touch someone, another to penetrate the spirit of the other. Only God who dwells within can be experienced at such an intimate and profound level. When we taste something, we usually consume it and transform it into ourselves; it becomes part of us.[12]

As we taste the Lord we want more and more of him, even as we keep going back to our favorite chocolate, as suggested in the psalmist's allusion of Abba's word being sweeter than honey. The spiritual senses reinforce the intimate connection with God that embraces both experience and understanding. Both dimensions are necessary in the work of paying attention to Abba and listening for his voice. Understanding is not sufficient in itself. We need to experience Abba in our inner person. The dimension of interiority is nurtured through tasting, touching, and smelling the soulful presence of Abba. As we give ourselves in love to God and desire to "taste and see that he is good," we draw closer with the one who created and knows us best. The practices of prayerful attention and heartfelt worship move us in the direction of spiritual union.

During recent teaching in Sucre, Bolivia, some of my Quechua and Aymara students told me that when they worship in Spanish they experience little intimacy with God; however, when they worship him in Quechua or Aymara their eyes fill with tears and they cry in joyful praise. The lyrical qualities of their mother tongues, with all the deep resonance and memories of their first language, release a flood of emotion and connectivity with

---

12. Keating, *Crisis of Faith, Crisis of Love*, 69.

An Invitation to Pay Attention

Abba. Paying close attention to the movements of Abba in our lives is like my students worshipping him in their birth languages. It helps us to perceive the subtleties of his ongoing, intimate presence leading us deeper into gratitude and love.

We return to the key question: How do we listen for Abba's voice in our lives? The answer begins in learning to pay attention to Abba's constant presence. We have to wake up, as St. Paul says, or come into awareness of what is the reality of our existence. Einstein famously declared, "God is found in the details." Yes! We are invited to wake up to God's presence in the details of our twenty-four-hour days. God wants to be known and to be in relationship with us. Our first step is to pay attention and to become aware of his loving presence. Awareness begins as an intentional action. After awareness, we move forward by concentrating and then questioning the matter at hand to come to a deeper appreciation of our subject. Finally, we respond by turning toward what we deem to be most important and then making our active choice. As we determine this choice in love, we fulfill the necessary steps of truly paying attention. Acting in love aligns our personal trajectory with the whispers of Abba by moving the clutter aside and making space for personal connection with the Spirit of God.

PART II—THE PRACTICE OF LISTENING

QUESTIONS FOR FURTHER REFLECTION

1. Distraction is a hurdle in coming to spiritual clarity. What are the main causes for distraction in your faith journey? What helps you to keep on track and resist the tendency to become distracted? In your journal write down what helps you to stay focused and share your findings with a spiritual friend. Perhaps he or she can share with you what helps to stay focused.

2. What simple steps help you to become aware of your personal surroundings and to pay attention to what is important?

3. Which of the five precepts related to paying attention are the most difficult for you to embrace? What dimensions come most naturally, and why do you think this is the case?

4. Make daily entries into your journal this week recording fresh observations as a result of paying close attention to your life. In what ways do these discoveries direct you to Abba? Have you understood something new about yourself because of these discoveries?

Chapter 9

A Journey in Time

As WE ATTEMPT TO come into awareness and pay attention to the details of our lives, we soon realize that everything we do happens in time, whether or not we are conscious of its passing. We were hiking on the wild West Coast Trail in the region of Ucluelet, Vancouver Island. It is a stunning walk along the rugged coast with wild surf, tall straight Sitka spruce, Douglas fir, western hemlock, massive western red cedar, plentiful bald eagles, and regular sightings of humpback whales, Pacific grey whales, and orcas cruising by. We walked slowly, enjoying the vistas in a reflective, quiet manner with an odd bit of commentary on what we were seeing or enjoying. Along the trail there were "artist loops" inviting hikers to closer vistas. On one such loop we enjoyed a close-up of a bald eagle preening its feathers, and on another we studied the regular blowhole exhaust of a meandering grey whale.

At the same time, we noted with interest that runners used the same trail (minus the artist loops) for their morning jog. Indeed, it was especially popular for young women with infants on their backs as a route for exercise and enjoyment of the fresh sea air. Two very different approaches were used to experience the same trail: one meditative, the other utilitarian; one for reflection, the other for bodily exercise; one slowly and mindfully, the other quickly with a focus on calories burned and the elevation of one's heart rate. Time passed in both the reflective walk and in the jogger's run, and from this perspective they were the same. However, what took place on an interior level was a very different experience. For some, the trail was a

PART II—THE PRACTICE OF LISTENING

way to appreciate the beauty of a majestic seascape and to enter an interior quiet that matched the holy environment; for the runners the trail was an intriguing path to log their ten thousand plus steps! The comparison raises the questions of how we both approach and use the time we are given. Is time something we merely pass through to achieve our goals or is time something we actually experience in and of itself?

CHRONOS AND KAIROS

The Greek New Testament has two words for time: *chronos* and *kairos*.[1] The word *chronos* has to do with clock time, as our word "chronology" suggests. *Chronos* speaks of twenty-four-hour clock time—hour by hour and minute by minute passing by in even sequence. Clock time suggests that we are simply moving from one event to another; time is seen as a flat dimension and we simply progress along a line. Understanding time in this manner depicts movement that can be routine. *Chronos* can also be sometimes marked with a degree of impatience as we look forward to some event in the future with a measure of frustration in the present.[2] We may be standing in line waiting to buy groceries or at the bank to pay a bill—in both cases impatient to get to the next event. The present is secondary, with the desire to be in a future superior time and place. Furthermore, *chronos* is often experienced with a measure of self-centeredness and lack of compassion as we rush by others in a hurried spirit to complete our tasks. A classic example of this attitude is seen in the story of the Good Samaritan (Luke 10:25–37), where the priest and the scribe cross to the other side of the street to avoid the injured man, while the Samaritan is willing to stop to assist the individual. Further, we are often distracted, with our minds focused on a future point and missing the importance and opportunities that exist in the now.[3]

The second Greek word, *kairos*, speaks of the "fullness of time" and the importance of the present moment. Paul uses the word in a variety of occasions, such as "making the most of the time" (Eph 5:16; Col 4:5). The Gospel writers also use *kairos*, such as at the beginning of Jesus' ministry: "Jesus came to Galilee, proclaiming the good news of God, and saying, 'The time is fulfilled, and the kingdom of God has come near; repent, and

1. See Hahn, "Chronos and Kairos."
2. See McNeill et al., *Compassion*, 92–100, on the role patience plays in one's spiritual journey.
3. See Tolle, *Power of Now*.

believe in the good news'" (Mark 1:14–15); and again in Jesus' warning to the people of Jerusalem: "But why do you not know how to interpret the present time?" (Luke 12:56). While we live in clock time—each of us having the same number of minutes and hours available to us—we can be alert to *kairos* moments that transform ordinary time. In each of these cases from the Scriptures the focus is on the importance of the present time as an opportunity to hear the voice of God and to discover what God is doing in that moment. Unfortunately, we are not very good at experiencing *kairos* time because of our impatience and our demand for instant gratification; we want things now and do not foster the ability to wait for the opportune moment. Just as we struggle to really listen, we are not always alert to discern the significance of what can be a God moment in our lives.

What helps us in the process of discerning *kairos* time? Two points can be instructive: first, we can look back and learn from the past. We hear Moses's call to "remember the long way that the Lord your God has led you" (Deut 8:2); or the psalmist's words, "My soul is cast down within me; therefore I remember you" (Ps 42:6); or the prophet Isaiah saying, "Remember the former things of old; for I am God, and there is no other" (Isa 46:9). Each of these injunctions encourages us to look back and see where God has acted for his people. In the same way we are invited to consider how God has acted in our lives and not to forget those special moments. They could be moments of conversion, baptism, or times we especially felt Abba's presence in our lives; we are invited to hold on to those moments and allow them to continually speak as we continue our journey of faith. We may find ourselves in arid times spiritually, but we can look back to our times of joy and enthusiasm in God's presence; or, like Isaiah hearing the call of God as a young man (Isa 6:8), we may reflect on our own mountaintop experience. These important times from the past can help us discern God's voice in the present.

A second help in discerning God's voice in the present is to look to the future with expectation. Jesus uses this technique to encourage his disciples when he is about to return to the Father, saying, "Do not let your heart's be troubled. . . . In my Father's house there are many dwelling places. If it were not so, would I have told you that I go to prepare a place for you?" (John 14:1–2). We also hear Paul's words to the Romans that God is able to transform our thinking and give us renovated minds to help us in our journey of faith (Rom 12:2). God is stronger than our fragility and he is able to sustain us amidst the struggles of life. Looking ahead with expectation helps us to realize that God is able to work in new ways in the present moment, and this hope stimulates fresh thinking and energy to persevere. Paul finishes his great work on hope by saying, "Therefore, my beloved, be steadfast, immovable, always excelling in the work of the Lord, because you know that in the Lord your labor is not in vain" (1 Cor 15:58). Here he shows the power of expectation and its value in propelling us forward in our immediate context.

When we are alert to *kairos* moments, we anticipate something new emerging out of our experience in the present moment. We learn to expect to hear a new word from God that speaks to our reality. Henri Nouwen points out the creative possibilities:

> *Kairos*, the other word for time, means opportunity to change your heart. There are as many opportunities to change your heart as there are events that you're part of. Everything is an opportunity to change your heart—a friend to visit, the museum, whatever, that's life. Looked upon from below, it's *chronos*; I have to survive, and I have to fight my way through it. Looked at from above, it is *kairos*; it's the opportunity to change your heart in everything you do.[4]

Nouwen suggests that the determining factor in dealing with time is our perception of it. If we merely wish to get through time it remains as simple *chronos*; however, if we understand time and the capacity it holds, we move into the sphere of *kairos*. It becomes alive and exciting, rich with the potential to blossom. *Kairos*, of course, does not mean that every moment is exhilarating. We would never survive such a condition! What it means is that we can receive each moment in all its fullness and live, not settling for a dull and unfulfilling existence.

A CONSIDERATION OF FAST AND SLOW TIMES

Our experience of *chronos* emerges from living fast lives. We often hurry from one event to another, not taking the time to enjoy the process of living. Sometimes we feel like we are on a treadmill; life is racing by and there is no opportunity to get off to rest. We move through our agenda for the day in a state of distraction, ticking off the items in a disconnected way with mere moments of respite when the bouncing balls find a place to rest. Living at such a fast pace prevents us from making much connection to the in-between moments of our day. It all becomes a blur, with only bits

---

4. Roderick, *Beloved*, 39.

A Journey in Time

coming into focus. We also miss much as we constantly look forward to the next experience. We postpone the now as we anticipate the preferred future moment coming down the line.

The invitation from God is always to come back to awareness and slow down to enjoy the existing moment in our lives. We can develop the skills of awareness and paying attention to the present moment. When we practice these skills we move out of fast time and begin to experience the present moment with its often surprising serendipities. Alice Walker speaks dramatically of moving out of the fast lane in her book *The Color Purple*:

> I think it pisses God off if you walk by the color purple in a field somewhere and don't notice it. People think pleasing God is all God cares about. But any fool in the world can see he is always trying to please us back . . . always making little surprises and springing them on us when we least expect it.[5]

The novelist is right. To enjoy the color purple in a field requires us to open our eyes and see what lies before us in the now.

We are invited to move from fast time and enter slow time. It is still *chronos* but we are moving off the treadmill and beginning to experience the point where we are at on the journey. In my own life the experiences of meditation and diving best illustrate the practice of slow time. When I meditate, each breath—each inhalation and exhalation—is felt in real time. Everything slows down as I focus on the breath coming in and going out. The mind settles, the heart relaxes, the body stills, the world stops spinning, and what is real in the moment rises to the surface. From this still place I listen for Abba's voice to gain his message through impressions in my body, mind, and spirit. My aim is twofold in this practice: both to listen now and to train myself to listen for God's voice when I resume the activities of the day.

A similar thing happens when I dive. The focus of inhalation and exhalation is highlighted in the exhaust of the regulator. I can actually hear each breath. This experience helps to slow the breathing process and time feels elongated. One of the dives I enjoy in Tobermory at the point of the Bruce Peninsula is a wreck of a ship lost in 1904, immersed deep beneath the water, lying upon a cliff face from bottom to top—the stern sitting at 150 feet and the remains of the midship at about 75 feet. I descend along a line from the surface to a point on the cliff where I connect with another

---

5. Walker, *Color Purple*, 196.

Part II—The Practice of Listening

line taking me to the wreck. The water is cold at 40 degrees Fahrenheit, but is a striking turquoise color—a diver's delight. Reaching the wreck, I slowly descend into the deeper, darker waters. Time slows down with each breath as the features of the shipwreck come into view: the boilers of the 1870 steamer at 115 feet, then the rail at 125 feet, and then finally the sand at 150 feet. Looking up at the wreck along the cliff face, I can read the name on the stern: *The Forest City*. I continue to hear my every breath, look at air and depth gauges to maintain controlled buoyancy, and enjoy the construction of the ship's wooden timbers—aware of the extreme silence of the underwater world. When the air level in the tank reduces to 750 PSI and the nitrogen levels in my blood stream reach the upper threshold, I make a slow ascent towards the surface to complete a safety stop at 15 feet for five minutes and then finally break the surface and make my way back to the dive vessel. The whole dive takes about 45 minutes of *chronos* time, but the experience feels like hours as every moment has been experienced in slow time.

Slow time of course is not simply about one's velocity. Moving at a calmer pace allows one to experience time in the moment rather than rushing and missing it. One spiritual guide uses the language of mindfulness when speaking of one's awareness of the present. He engages a water image to portray this sense of awareness:

> When you see only waves, you might miss the water. But if you are mindful, you will be able to touch the water within the waves as well. Once you are capable of touching the water, you will not mind the coming and going of the waves. You are no longer concerned about the birth and the death of the wave. You are no longer afraid. You are no longer upset about the beginning or the end of the wave, or that the wave is higher or lower, more or less beautiful. You are capable of letting these ideas go because you have already touched the water.[6]

Touching the water means connecting with the present moment in a manner that reveals its essence. When we move from fast time and experience slow time we open ourselves to the potential of *kairos*, which becomes the time of opportunity.

---

6. Nhat Hanh, *Living Buddha, Living Christ*, 157.

A Journey in Time

KAIROS: THE TIME OF OPPORTUNITY

The Old Testament presents a deep sense of *kairos* time. It first comes to us in the celebration of the three annual feasts of Passover, Pentecost and Sukkot. In these weeklong celebrations the people of Israel were invited to travel to Jerusalem and remember the great works of God amongst the nation.[7] One author writes of these celebrations in relation to time: "It has its basis in an appreciation of time and the refusal simply to accept continuous repetition without a break."[8] The people took a week out of their schedule three times a year to come together and focus on the saving activities of Yahweh—even while the surrounding cultures were caught up in the repetition of the daily grind.

Another aspect of *kairos* time was the weekly marking of the Sabbath. For the Israelites time was not experienced as flat time where each day rolled over to the next without any significant change. For the Israelites time was seen as cyclical, whereby every seventh day the people ceased from all work and experienced rest while worshiping Yahweh. The two passages that record the Decalogue (the Ten Commandments) present different reasons for celebrating the Sabbath. The first reminds the people that resting on the seventh day is a creation mandate to imitate the resting of God after the work of creation (Exod 20:8–11); as God rested so the people are to stop all of their work and be refreshed on the seventh day. The second recording of the Decalogue presents the redemption of Israel from the bondage of Egypt as the basis for the celebration of the Sabbath. The people have been liberated from a life of slavery; therefore they are to break out of the routine and rejoice before God on the Sabbath day (Deut 5:12–15). Instead of viewing time continuously, Israel experienced time as a cycle in which a day of rest followed every six days of work. Abraham Heschel describes the power of this perspective: "In the tempestuous ocean of time and toil there are islands of stillness where man may enter a harbour and reclaim his dignity. The island is the seventh day, the Sabbath, a day of detachment from things, instruments and practical affairs as well as of attachment to the spirit."[9] He goes on to say that the "Sabbaths are our cathedrals in time," making time as important as place in one's experience of life and faith.[10]

---

7. See Chapter 7 for more on the feasts.
8. Mayer, "Feast, Passover," 632.
9. Heschel, *I Asked for Wonder*, 35.
10. Ibid., 36.

Hence, both the festivals and the Sabbath mark out seasons of *kairos* that provide opportunities for fresh action and deeper connection with Abba.

The Sabbath also reminds us that we are worth our own time. It reminds us that we are free to be what God has called us to become and that we are liberated to realize the vision that God has for us.[11] *Kairos* invites us to explore time in its deepest profundity, enabling us to see clearly and to act with true insight in the moment. In the film *All Is Lost*, a man is adrift on a life raft in the southern Indian Ocean 1,700 miles from the Sumatra Straits. Eight days pass and hope for rescue wanes. Out of water and food, he writes a note, "I have tried my best but all is lost," and puts it in a bottle and releases it into the sea. When he sees the light of a ship on the horizon, in one final act he starts a fire on the raft with his journal pages to signal the distant boat. When the raft has burned to nothing and he is forced off to escape the flames, he now floats in the sea under a starry night sky, looking at the distant light. He has done everything he can—either he is seen or he dies. As he sinks into the sea, still looking up, a hand breaks the surface and he is able to swim towards his rescuer's embrace. In the *kairos* moment he acts with insight and by risking all is rewarded with rescue and life.

The *kairos* moment teaches us to wait like the sailor for his final chance. In the Scriptures we see Job having to wait as he works out his pain after losing his family and comes to terms with the loss. David waits for years to claim his kingship under the threat of King Saul even though it has been promised to him through the prophet Samuel. Even Jesus has to wait for thirty years living and working in the small town of Nazareth before launching out to begin his public ministry. Perhaps Keating is correct when he suggests, "There is nothing so humbling as waiting—that is why time was created, so that we might learn to wait."[12] *Kairos* emerges out of slow time accompanied with a spirit of waiting so that the moment of opportunity flashes forth and the right action can be taken. The apostle Paul alludes to this combination when he writes, "But when the fullness of time had come, God sent his son" (Gal 4:4). The Son's "day in the light," as Annie Dillard so elegantly phrases it, came nigh and he graced the world with his saving presence under a Bethlehem night sky.[13]

---

11. See Farrell, *Father Is Very Fond of Me*, 87.
12. Keating, *Crisis of Faith*, 38.
13. Dillard, *For the Time Being*, 45.

A Journey in Time

THE INTERSECTION OF TIME AND DISCIPLINE

Listening to anyone requires one to quit talking, slow down, and focus on what the other person is saying. The same is true in self-understanding. If we are always rushing we will not be able to reflect clearly on our own thoughts or actions. Hurry creates a spirit of distraction, and multitasking divides and fosters muddled thinking. Kierkegaard uses the example of a person trying to look in a mirror while running; it is impossible to continuously see a jarring image.[14] One has to stop and carefully look to view clearly and understand one's own reflection. As we slow down we have greater awareness of our thoughts and actions. We do not simply react but think through what is best in each situation. For example, if someone cuts us off while driving and we respond with an angry exclamation or hand sign then our action is simply a reaction; it would be better to avoid the other car, remain calm, and breathe deeply, so that a further action does not lead to an accident or a sparring exchange of road rage.

What helps us to slow down and not simply react in a thoughtless manner? What disciplines can shift us from mere reaction to nurturing a thoughtful, life-enhancing response? What activities can be shaped into disciplines that help us slow down in conscious time, fostering clarity and revealing *kairos* moments in our lives? How can we reject our tendency to see time as continuous and flat, and instead, celebrate a cyclical view of time?

To begin, meditation, centering prayer, and reflection on the Scriptures are obvious practices that can assist us in moving from *chronos* to *kairos* time. At the same time, there may be other ways to supplement these disciplines, which we all are invited to discover. Evelyn Underhill reminds us that we all have to work our own spiritual muscles and find the spiritual exercises that are effective for us: "The first thing we have to find out is the kind of practice that suits our souls—ours, not someone else's, and now, at this stage of its growth."[15] What is helpful for us may not be for you, so you have to discover your own exercises in "working out your salvation with fear and trembling" (Phil 2:12). A friend of ours goes on a monthly retreat in order to slow down and nurture a contemplative spirit; another gardens; we take walks, hike trails, and seek out opportunities to take road trips. There are many possibilities for increasing the capacity of living with awareness. The salient point is the discovery and practice of the disciplines,

---

14. Kierkegaard, *Purity of Thought*, 108.
15. Underhill, *Concerning the Inner Life*, 39.

for simple ideas will not change our method of reacting when our buttons are pushed. Again, as mentioned in an earlier chapter, a practice needs to be developed to change one's responses at the "epidermal or surface level"; otherwise, the old behavior patterns prevail.[16]

THE INTERSECTION OF TIME AND LISTENING FOR GOD

On Signal Hill in St. John's, Newfoundland, overlooking the harbor entrance where fortifications have been standing since the 1760s, there is a museum marking the first transatlantic wireless transmission from Cornwall, England, by Guglielmo Marconi on December 12, 1901. Marconi demonstrated for the first time that radio signals could be transported over large distances—in this case, 1,700 miles from the transmitter. To accomplish this feat Marconi had to overcome much resistance and unbelief from the scientific community, forging ahead independently to determine the necessary apparatus, signals, location, and support gear to complete the experiment. It required a great deal of perseverance to put it all together to finally hear the rewarding "pop, pop, pop" in the rudimentary headsets. His work was ultimately recognized, of course, as it revolutionized communications at land and on sea, and for which he was awarded the Nobel Prize for physics in 1909. When we visited the site, seeing photographs of his early work impressed us on a number of levels: his vision of what could take place, his persistence amidst significant resistance, his detailed fine-tuning to achieve the proper signal and experience success. We can learn many things from reflecting on his work, but on a spiritual plane one thing especially becomes clear: as Marconi kept revisiting his calibrations to achieve the proper signal so also do we need to keep dialing in to capture the nuances of the Holy Spirit as we live our lives. There is a need to keep listening, keep focusing, so the subtle whispers of Abba are heard and given importance in our journeys in time.

In this process of listening we transform our view of time. Time is not our enemy or a taskmaster to be feared, creating a sense of gloom—"I'm turning thirty today and am no longer young"; "I've turned fifty and now I will be seen as over the hill"; "I am sixty-five and they are putting me out to pasture." These thoughts depict how our culture views time as "it chews us up and spits us out with appalling ease," but they do not present

---

16. See Willard, *Divine Conspiracy*, 358.

a biblical understanding of it.[17] Rather, as Kathleen Norris enjoins, we put on a different lens: "But the monastic perspective welcomes time as a gift from God, and seeks to put it to good use rather than allowing us to be used up by it."[18] This gift of time becomes a tool enabling us to connect with God. As we slow down in time and pay attention to our daily experience we become aware of his quiet whispers and respectful voice. In the actual moment God reveals himself to us if we are receptive and listening for his words. Consequently, it is important for us to befriend time and see it as our ally and not as a tyrannical overlord.

We recognize that there are seasons in our lives where time is viewed differently. In our youth we feel that time is endless and that there is an abundance of moments to strike out on any path we desire. As we approach forty we wonder if we are going to achieve our goals or not. As we enter our seventies we may feel that there is nothing left to look forward to. All of these perspectives place an undo emphasis on *chronos* at the expense of *kairos* time. The reality is that *kairos* awaits us at any age! Seniors may have more time to connect with God than ever before and experience increased opportunities for service and expressing Christ's compassion. Certainly young parents have full schedules, but the possibility of *kairos* moments abound for receptive persons as they pay attention to the amazing creativity of their children and the opportunities for engagement and growth that flow from it. Abba gives us time as a gift that we are to unwrap carefully as we would a precious gift from a loved one, one fold at a time with intentionality and awareness. As we pass through *chronos* we are able to move from fast to slow time and periodically embrace the gift of *kairos*. In these moments, if we are listening carefully, Abba's voice is heard, new doors open, and fresh possibilities are awakened. We have our time under the sun to open up to God's love and say yes to his overtures. Time is our friend to be embraced and used for the glory of God. Time as *kairos* is a sign of the kingdom of God presenting the continuing new work of his creation.

---

17. Norris, *The Cloister Walk*, 19.
18. Ibid., 19.

PART II—THE PRACTICE OF LISTENING

QUESTIONS FOR FURTHER REFLECTION

1. Do you see time as an enemy or a friend? Write down in your journal why this is the case.

2. What are your ways of managing *chronos* time so that stress, hurry, and the urgent do not shape your schedule? Name the coping strategies you use or can use to gain control of your day's events.

3. How and when have you experienced *kairos* time in your life? Write in your journal or share with a friend how these moments unfolded.

4. We listen for God's voice in the dimension of time. Moving from fast to slow time gives us a better opportunity for hearing from Abba instead of remaining in a state of distraction and frenzy. What practices help you to be in the moment so that *kairos* clarity has a role in your journey with God?

Chapter 10

Service and Sacrifice as the Downward Way

IN HIS FIRST PUBLIC sermon in the synagogue of Nazareth, Jesus announces that he comes to bring good news to the poor, powerless, sick, and marginalized of society. By citing the words of Isaiah he proclaims that he has been anointed by the Spirit of the Lord "to bring good news to the poor, recovery of sight to the blind, to let the oppressed go free, and to proclaim the year of the Lord's favor" (Luke 4:16–21). Through this powerful proclamation Jesus establishes the direction of his ministry to be focused primarily on the voiceless ones of the earth and not the rich, powerful, and privileged. In his sermon he provides us with a path to follow for living and for treating the fragile ones of our communities. We are to love them even as we love ourselves. The overarching theme of our lives is "to love God and love our neighbor."

A beautiful example of this approach is presented in the documentary *The Drop Box*, portraying the work of Pastor Lee Jong-rak in Jusarang Community Church ("God's Love" Community) in Seoul, South Korea. As a response to abandoned babies left to die in the backstreets of the city, Pastor Lee builds a drop box connected to his church to encourage desperate mothers who have no options to place their babies in it rather than leaving them to die in the streets. After providing immediate care he arranges for the babies to be placed in care facilities to be adopted by others in the future. Many of the babies have disabilities such as Down syndrome, missing limbs, or other illnesses, and hence are devalued or seem to require too much care.

Part II—The Practice of Listening

Pastor Lee and his wife have saved over five hundred babies from certain death. Furthermore, they have adopted fifteen little ones with physical and intellectual challenges to be their own children and are dedicating their lives to their care. Throughout the film they explain that they are not choosing this path to be heroes or martyrs but are simply following the downward way of service towards the broken and hurting of society as modeled by Jesus. Pastor Lee's final words in the documentary explain his devotion to the little ones of the drop box, reminding us of Abba's love for each one of us: "The reason I became their father was that God has adopted me."

THE DOWNWARD WAY

In his letter to the Philippians Paul provides the logic for the life of service and sacrifice as he exhorts the church: "Do nothing from selfish ambition or conceit, but in humility regard others as better than yourselves. Let each of you look not to your own interests, but to the interests of others" (2:3–4). The immediate context for these imperatives is the specter of division in the community of faith at Philippi as opponents of the true gospel proclaim their distorted variations (1:15–17, 28). Paul is encouraging the church to follow a path of love, listening, and understanding as they work through the challenges of the competing positions. They are not to simply fall into divisive groups but to keep striving together in love so that the church of Christ is built up and not torn down. In his argument Paul uses the peculiar phrase "in humility regard others as better than yourselves" (1:3b), which can be initially misunderstood. He is not advocating becoming a doormat and allowing others to take advantage; rather, it is more like allowing someone to move ahead of you in a line, acting from a perspective of confidence where one chooses to express grace to another person and offer a position of strength.[1]

As Paul develops his argument he encourages the church to take on the mind of Christ as they interact with one another (2:5). The words "let the same mind be in you" are captured in the Greek word *phroneō*, which has the meaning of "intellect, perspective, point of view, a way of looking at life."[2] As a result, they are not to simply follow their own instincts or the mores of contemporary Hellenistic culture, but to follow the model Jesus provided. Paul develops this servant paradigm by relating through

1. See Palmer, *Integrity*, 90–1.
2. Ibid., 94. See also Arndt and Gingrich, 874.

a liturgical hymn the downward sweep of Christ's existence (2:6–11). The poem begins by acknowledging Christ's pre-existent status as "being in the form of God" (v. 6), emptying himself of divine glory to take on the form of human nature (v. 7), and descending in obedience to the point of death on a cross for our sake (v. 8). This direction downward represents Jesus' commitment to give up his rights for the well-being—in fact, salvation—of those who are receptive to God's voice. He dies so that we might live. He suffers so that we might gain eternal life.

The path of the hymn pivots at this juncture towards ascension, declaring that because of Christ's humility and sacrifice he now gains the name that is above every name, including exaltation, from "every knee in heaven and on earth and under the earth," and that every tongue will confess that he is Lord (vv. 9–11). Consequently, the liturgical hymn presented by Paul speaks of the pre-existence, existence, and post-existence of Christ, engaging the image of descending to earth and ascending to glory after his work on earth is completed. The result of Christ's journey is that, as Craddock points out, "there is no place in the universe, no created being, beyond the reach of the redeeming act of the servant Christ. God's act is the vindication of what the hymn has declared: The central event in the drama of salvation is an act of humble service."[3]

It is amazing that the apostle Paul writes or employs this profound liturgical hymn portraying the mystical work of Christ to address the mundane Christian struggle of maintaining unity and an attitude of service for one another. It could be seen as an overly dramatic response to a rather banal issue—a poetic masterpiece addressing the problem of people getting along. On the other hand, such a use of the hymn indicates the importance of unity in the faith community and expressions of service and sacrifice as endemic to the way of following Christ. Paul is emphasizing that it is not sufficient to engage a self-referential system for making choices and establishing personal values. The world does not revolve around us. When we live in a system of competing needs where each person pursues his or her own interests, we parallel the days of the judges when "there was no king in Israel; and all the people did what was right in their own eyes" (Judg 21:25). Things did not end well for God's people then. When the reference point is oneself—one's personal desires—the end is ultimately chaos, confusion, and unhappiness.

---

3. Craddock, *Philippians*, 42.

Part II—The Practice of Listening

For Paul it is imperative that the believing community have the mind of Christ, centered on love and personal sacrifice. When we embrace Christ's point of view—his "mind"—we share his passion for both love of God and love of neighbor. When we breathe this atmosphere of sacrifice we echo the model that enhances the lives of others, our community, and the larger world—our common home.

SERVICE IN ORDINARY TIME

When we broaden our reference point for living to include others, we open up to the possibilities of service in the ordinariness of life. The theologian Karl Rahner describes the centrality of the downward way: "No member of the Mystical Body of Christ is alive for himself or herself alone. Each has a function of service to perform for the others, even for those members who are still merely 'potential.'"[4] Rahner is encouraging us to see the core of our mission as the heart of service—"the Christian as Christian"—expressing Christ in our service to all others, whether they be in the community of faith or not. This path of sacrifice becomes concrete in its intersection with time as ordinary events of the day provide opportunities to offer service for Christ. As we yield to Jesus we offer ourselves to him in unexpected encounters that arise throughout the day. The popular expression "spontaneous acts of kindness" (i.e., buying coffee for the folk behind you at the drive through) is one way of visualizing the selfless offering of kindness. But it is in the concrete dimensions of the day that we offer ourselves in service: parents taking the time to be patient and loving with their children in the commotion of making daily lunches; managers serving their staff by helping them understand new computer software; friends offering support to listen when life becomes hectic; neighbors helping grumpy neighbors by bringing in their garbage cans.

Service in time is seen primarily in unspectacular ways. In his essential book on building community, *Life Together*, Bonhoeffer lists a variety of ways of serving, unspectacular in themselves, but helpful in walking with others. He elevates serving in his choosing of the word "ministry": the ministry of holding one's tongue, the ministry of meekness, the ministry of listening, the ministry of helpfulness, the ministry of bearing, the ministry of proclaiming, the ministry of authority.[5] As an example, Bonhoeffer

---

4. Rahner, *The Practice of Faith*, 102.
5. Bonhoeffer, *Life Together*, 91–109.

Service and Sacrifice as the Downward Way

describes the service of helping as "simple assistance in trifling, external matters. . . . Nobody is too good for the meanest service."[6] Certainly in a faith community there are opportunities for this kind of unspectacular ministering: cleaning, moving tables and chairs, emptying dishwashers, making repairs, garden work, giving rides, taking out the trash. In our century-old church site the list of needs for the service of helps is long. Without this ongoing engagement of service confusion ensues and ministry falters.

As another example of service, Bonhoeffer speaks to the ministry of "bearing your brother or sister," by which he means suffering and enduring the irritating Christian. He develops this aspect of sacrifice saying, "The freedom of the other person includes . . . his weaknesses and oddities, which are such a trial to our patience, everything that produces frictions, conflicts, and collisions among us." Bonhoeffer does not stop there in his understanding of this sacrifice: "To bear the burden of the other person means involvement with the created reality of the other, to accept and affirm it, and, in bearing with it, to break through to the point where we take joy in it."[7] To understand that quirky or annoying individuals are actually opportunities for engagement in ministry transforms the effort. As we bear with others we strengthen both the church and our own spiritual character, and provide opportunities for the brother or sister to grow in faith.

Sacrifice also becomes a touchstone for those who are searching for a deeper purpose in life. Individuals who are becoming turned off by our competitive, materialistic, self-serving culture are looking for another way—one that draws the world together rather than dividing and instilling brokenness. Through sacrifice people encounter a place that penetrates their hardness and moves them closer to hope. The community center Frontlines, established by our church twenty-five years ago, continues to attract not only youth and children who need love and attention, but also people of power who want to serve the community through it. The weakness and humility of the outreach touches a place in the hearts of individuals, drawing them to an attitude of service to the poor. This movement towards service resonates with the deeper currents of our lives where we have an attraction to foster integration and growth in those who move around us—a human form of nuclear fusion. We become, as Catherine Doherty says, "God's icebreakers . . . who bring light, and fire and warmth into the cold and ever more mechanical world of tomorrow where everyone is treated

6. Ibid., 99.
7. Ibid., 101.

'efficiently.'"[8] Doherty describes our service with such a delicate metaphor! "We are being chosen to enter into the loneliness of modern humanity, that ice age of tomorrow, and become God's icebreakers and inns for all the wounded and frozen ones, so that they might be thawed out by our love."[9] Who would not want to participate?

SERVICE AS CARE

We begin to understand the power of caring when we recognize that we also will one day be in need of it. When we are strong we live with the illusion that we will never change and that caring is always for someone else. Yet as we open our eyes and see the truth of our own aging, we acknowledge that there is coming a time when we will need the service of others. This insight is valuable as it keeps us connected with other people and especially our community of faith. We have the opportunity to reach out and provide service to others now, but the time is coming when we will be dependent on the beneficence of family, friends, and caregivers we do not know. For caring to take place we need to make space in our lives for others. If our lives are overly packed with things to do, projects to accomplish, trips to take, purchases to buy, and anxious thoughts for the future, then there is little room for the person in need. Very quickly we become like the preoccupied priest or scribe who scurries along with no time for the dying man on the side of the road (Luke 10:31–32). As we open up our lives, we allow the vulnerable a place in it, and room for compassion grows. We stop seeing the needy person as an irritant that gets in our way, and start to see her as a fellow traveler in the cycle of life. "It is this compassion that can make us live many lives, the lives of the young as well as the lives of the old," write Nouwen and Gaffney, describing this welcoming perspective. "Every time we allow another person into our desert and learn to speak his or her language, we live our lives together and deepen each other's humanity."[10] And as we embrace this path of compassion, as the authors continue, we see that "we are for others."[11] We become present to the other person so that their story is heard and their life is valued.

---

8. Doherty, *Poustinia*, 153.
9. Ibid.
10. Nouwen and Gaffney, *Aging*, 115.
11. Ibid., 117.

Service and Sacrifice as the Downward Way

In our own church context I am blessed to work with two associate pastors who model and practice this spirit of valuing and embracing all others regardless of station in life. These true shepherds reinforce the reality of Abba's acceptance and proclamation that life is precious and worthwhile in every person who graces the doors of our faith community—whether it be strangers who need assistance, shut-ins seeking the Communion elements, or isolated and lonely individuals in need of conversation living in the high-rise towers of Weston.

SERVICE AS SENT ONES

The inspiring challenge of the Christian journey is the truth that every follower of Jesus has a vocation to partner with God. Jesus puts it this way: "Very truly, I tell you, whoever receives one whom I send receives me; and whoever receives me receives him who sent me" (John 13:20). Jesus is the sender and we are the sent ones. We are sent to be his light and love to all those whom we meet and serve. It is not the sole domain of the clergy or professionals; rather it is a requirement for every Christian to enter into the downward path of service and love. Van Breemen clarifies the obligation: "We understand that in the church every Christian is sent . . . we are all called to labor in communion with Christ. This implies liberation from egocentrism and an opening up to Jesus. This kind of mission is essential for the church and for each person in the church."[12] We all are asked to embrace a life of self-giving where the other person is valued and cared for no matter what their circumstances.

To engage in this life practice, we need to keep our eyes constantly on Christ. Then our hands remain open to receive his calling and our ministry and mission remain energized and alive with the Spirit's presence and touch. As we freely accept this vocation of love we experience the synergy of the triune God working within us. Alone we are not sufficient for the ongoing task of demonstrating kindness to a broken world, for over time we are broken by the crushing demands of life. However, as we open ourselves to the Spirit's leading, Abba works thorough us to bring fruitfulness to our humble offerings of service. As we take on this new second nature of "Christ in us" we become his hands and feet for touching others and revealing the coming kingdom of God. We become his ambassadors, in the words of the apostle Paul, and are his representatives for revealing the love, words, and actions of

12. Van Breemen, *Let All God's Glory Through*, 44.

God. The authors of *Compassion* clarify our purpose: "The Christian life is a life of witnessing through servanthood to the compassionate God, not a life in which we seek suffering and pain."[13] We express his healing presence to the lives we touch in our compassionate service. It is not simply about service or activism but about entering into the ongoing ministry of Jesus, who encounters individuals through our words and actions.

Representing Jesus to others is our deepest calling and is the root of our compassionate presence in the world. We can actually touch others with God's personal love so that they might spiritually blossom through his felt presence. In our own community we think of Matthew, who as a child ran the streets of Weston and who by his own admission was involved in nefarious activities. He was drawn to Frontlines by the charity of Pastor Bonnie, who at that time directed the center. Her love, patience, and continual acceptance penetrated his heart with the love of Jesus, drawing him to become his follower. Today Matthew is a chef by trade, and also sits on the governing board of the community center, helping to provide leadership for the organization (which now has a chef's training program from which his younger brother recently graduated!). He desires to live as a conduit of Jesus before his young family, colleagues, faith community, and broader community of Weston. Touched by Jesus' love through Bonnie and others at Frontlines, he has now has come full circle, demonstrating a similar expression of God's love through the same ministry to one of the poorest communities in the province of Ontario.

SERVICE AND LISTENING FOR GOD'S VOICE

The first step in merging the themes of service and listening for God's voice is to intentionally begin where we are: if we are raising young children we attempt to hear God's voice amidst the constant demands of child rearing; if we are in the midst of the power years we serve others through our interactions rather than seeking our own ascendency; if we are in the senior years we take the time and opportunity to listen to others who are in pain or isolation. There are places of service in our immediate context—in a marriage relationship or a single's life, as a member of a work crew or team, or as a teacher or student; whatever the situation, the invitation is to travel the downward way of service wherever we find ourselves. There may open up in the future opportunities to serve elsewhere, but the essential

13. McNeill et al., *Compassion*, 30.

Service and Sacrifice as the Downward Way

thing is to begin in the now and in one's present environment. The Hebrew language suggests such an approach to life by not having a word for "obey," but employing the word "to hear or to listen" (Deut 6:4), often coupling it with the word "today" (as in "hear today" in Ps 95:7), to engender the idea of obedience.[14] We are invited to keep "listening-hearing" for Abba's voice and to do this amidst the daily demands of life. It is not necessary to seek or serve in more glamorous contexts but to focus our desire to serve in the hard realities of our immediate life situation. Jean Vanier's decision to begin his service to the disabled and intellectually challenged began with two men he knew.[15] Slowly over time the ministry grew into L'Arche, which now has hundreds of communities worldwide serving those with intellectual disabilities. He simply began where he was by taking two men into his home and caring for them.

So listening begins where we are and often with some form of displacement—the context where we feel displaced to some degree by the daily grind. We are stretched or pulled apart at some level in our service, like a mother feeling challenged by the constant needs of little children or the middle generation feeling the simultaneous demands of adult children and aging parents. As we experience these or similar situations with a sacrificial spirit rather than fleeing from them, we embrace the downward model of Jesus that fosters a listening heart. The authors of *Compassion* describe this response as "voluntary displacement," where "we cast off the illusion of 'having it together' and thus begin to experience our true condition, which is that we, like everyone else, are pilgrims on the way, sinners in need of grace."[16] They offer hope in the meaning of this experience: "Voluntary displacement leads us to the existential recognition of our inner brokenness and thus brings us to a deeper solidarity with the brokenness of our fellow human beings."[17] Hence, we are called to identify and embrace these places of displacement, because it is in the uncomfortable spaces where we often discover the presence of God and hear from him most distinctly.

Displacement calls us to live with an attitude of patience. Service happens over the long haul; it is "a long obedience in the same direction," as suggested by Eugene Peterson.[18] It is not limited to a short-term mission trip

---

14 Austel, "Shamah," 938.
15. Vanier, "Seeing God in Others."
16. McNeill et al., *Compassion*, 63–64.
17. Ibid., 64.
18. Peterson, *Long Obedience in the Same Direction*.

where we are in and out of a place of need in two weeks and then back to living comfortable lives. Sacrifice calls us to live patiently and "to enter actively into the thick of life and to fully bear the suffering within and around us."[19] As the root of the word *pati* ("suffer") suggests, so we are invited to embrace the suffering that our displacement holds. There is a call to pay attention to the very stress points that we may be trying to escape. What is God saying to us in our point of pain? Too often we simply want to get through our hurt and return to our safe lives, missing the opportunity that hardship offers us for transformation. Can we stay with the moment of challenge to find the light that is offered from within the darkness? Patience allows us to experience what we need to experience before the page turns and the story continues. Meditation teaches us that pain eventually disperses, but we have to allow it time to do its work in the journey toward wholeness.

In sacrifice, service, and suffering God shows up in our lives. In these times we are closer to the cleansing holy fire than in the times of repose. If our desire is to hear from God than we need to pay attention during these uncomfortable times. The very moments we wish away can be the burning coals offered by the seraphim to transform us (see Isa 6:6). Receive the downward moments. Receive the possibilities for service. Receive the opportunities for sacrifice as ways of linking with the downward but enlivening presence of Jesus. Donald English summarizes this descending path as "the true path of discipleship, not the permanently clear, bright and shining way but the lowly path of service, or rejection, or persecution." In the process we are "discovering daily the joy that is found not necessarily in happy circumstances but in faithful service and daily rising with him."[20] May we be listening for Abba's whisper as we embrace times of service, for in giving to others we receive the self-giving of the Father, who travels with us in solidarity through his Son Jesus.

19. McNeill et al., *Compassion*, 93.
20. English, *Message of Mark*, 241.

Service and Sacrifice as the Downward Way

QUESTIONS FOR FURTHER REFLECTION

1. In your daily activities what forms of service frequent your life? How are these experiences an opportunity to travel the downward way of Christ?

2. Caring for others can become a way of learning about ourselves. In light of this observation, write down three or four ways that caring for individuals has shaped your own spiritual path.

3. Is there a dimension in your life of being "a sent one" that has revealed opportunities for service and sacrifice? Write down what that area is and describe in a few paragraphs how being sent connects you with serving others.

4. In *The Problem of Pain* C. S. Lewis suggests, "God shouts in our pains."[21] How have you found this to be true in your own faith journey? Have there been times where you have discerned Abba's direction in moments of dislocation? Describe one of these times to a friend and reflect together on what you can bring forward from that experience that potentially informs your present situation.

5. We are invited to listen for God's voice in the unexpected moments of service and personal sacrifice. As you reflect on this theme can you identify times when Abba has spoken to you while offering service? What have you learned from God during those times?

21. Lewis, *Problem of Pain*, 93.

Chapter 11

Light within the Struggle of Diminishment

Jean Vanier describes the passage of life as a voyage from "the womb to the tomb."[1] In the opening episode of his acclaimed series for Vision TV, "Images of Love, Words of Hope," he describes the fragility of the child's early years. The child is completely in the hands of the mother and father for survival and development and remains in such a position of reliance throughout her childhood. As the child grows into adolescence and adulthood there is an increasing movement to strength and independence. The middle years of life are characterized by power and self-determination with expansion in terms of resources, wisdom, education, and experience. These are the years of accomplishment, respect, and recognition, elevating one's sense of social standing and prominence. As the years move toward retirement and beyond, there is a return to fragility in aging, sickness, loss of income, and dwindling opportunities. The loss begins slowly, often through sickness and declining resources, but increases as one declines in health in body and mind. The onslaught of cancer, diabetes, and Alzheimer's vividly demonstrates the final road of diminishment for the person who once enjoyed the middle years of power.

How does Abba continue to speak during the reality of diminishment? If the life journey is cast in the mould Vanier has described, then how does God show up during the decline? In considering these questions we turn our attention to passages from the Bible that frame the descending path we all face.

1 Vanier, "Mystery of Being and Growth."

Light within the Struggle of Diminishment

INEVITABILITY OF DIMINISHMENT

In the pastoral epistles Paul writes to his younger charges to encourage them in the ongoing work of establishing the churches in Christ. Paul exhorts Timothy to "be strong in the grace that is in Christ Jesus" (2 Tim 2:1), which parallels his earlier exhortation "to rekindle the gift of God that is within you" (1:6). Both statements encourage Timothy "to stir up" in an intentional manner the faith that he has been called to. As the embers of a fire need to be stirred periodically to increase the flame, so Paul adjures Timothy to remain vibrant in his commitment to Jesus. It is too easy to become distracted with other voices and to lose interest in one's principle vocation; therefore the apostle encourages him to live a disciplined life as exemplified by the soldier (2 Tim 2:4), the athlete (2 Tim 2:5), and a hardworking farmer (2 Tim 2:2–6).

Within this passage Paul further exhorts Timothy to "share in suffering like a good soldier of Christ Jesus" (2 Tim 2:3), that is, to identify with Jesus in his sufferings and not simply in his glory (Phil 3:10). Paul proceeds to describe Jesus' own suffering in the creedal-like statement, "Remember Jesus Christ, raised from the dead, a descendent of David—that is my gospel" (2 Tim 2:8), and also details his own suffering as one being chained like a common criminal in a Roman cell (vv. 9–10). Suffering is presented as part of the reality in the journey of faith. Timothy is not to be ashamed of Jesus' or Paul's sufferings even though they are not understood by the general public. (The Jewish community saw Christ's death on the cross as blasphemous in terms of his role as Messiah, and the Greek community understood the theme of the resurrection as foolishness.) Rather than being ashamed of suffering, or what we are naming "diminishment," the apostle Paul avers that the movement from life to death and back to life is the sequence for everything. All of creation is marked by the cycle of disintegration and new life. Paul articulates this reality in the hymn fragment that closes the unit: "If we have died with him, we will also live with him; if we endure, we will also reign with him; if we deny him, he will also deny us; if we are faithless, he remains faithful—for he cannot deny himself (vv. 11–13). Diminishment and suffering are not surprising factors but essential components of the life process, as even Christ himself suffered and experienced death prior to new life. As Christ suffered so we travel a similar path, but it ends with new life and not with destruction as Paul claims.

Paul reminds Timothy that decline is part of the human condition. It is inevitable and awaits us all no matter how strong we are at any given point. Yet the mystery remains that new life emerges from the ashes. In Christ, chaos and death are not the end, but simply doors to pass through into resurrection life. We observe the movement toward decline and new life every day if we have eyes to see it. When forests go up in flames, new growth emerges from the ashes in record time; when bodies decay, nutrients of life are given back into the earth and the soil and small life are enriched; when stars explode, energy and gases are flung into space, ultimately creating new stars and galaxies. The way of diminishment is the basis for all life and holds forth mysteries to amaze us if we recognize its power for life rather than dwell on the past and its fleeting glory. It is this connection between the downward way and new life that Paul opens up to Timothy that we must recognize; otherwise we are drawn into cynicism, anger, and fear. When we accept this movement we live with a greater degree of grace, gentleness, and humor, and receive the turning of life's wheel with greater patience, hope, and strength.

CHALLENGES OF DIMINISHMENT

As we recognize the inevitability of our decline we also understand that it includes a dimension of suffering, and a first sign of its impact is a measure of isolation. It may raise its head in the form of aches and pains that restricts one's previous forms of activity, social engagement, and enjoyment of life. For example, a friend injures a knee and is unable to keep playing hockey, which is a personal passion of theirs. The issue is not just the absence of participating in the game but also missing out on the social interactions around the team's activities. Another person loves singing but over time develops a node on her vocal cords that restricts a successful singing career. Again, it is not only the end of making music but also the restriction of creative working relationships. Recently, at our church facility our elevator broke down, which proved to be a complicated problem to solve due to new safety standards and significant costs. As a result, the elevator was out of commission for several weeks, impacting a number of folk in our community. People who regularly enjoyed weekly worship were now unable to attend because they could not safely enter the sanctuary. The felt experience was one of isolation for the individuals who were separated from the community that holds them up.

Related to the dimension of isolation is a growing sense of sadness as one is cut off from companions who may also be experiencing a degree of diminishment. Timothy, the apostle Paul's dear friend, experiences a degree of desolation as he hears that his beloved mentor is anticipating an imminent death. He will be left alone with the responsibilities to shape the church in Ephesus without the wisdom and support of his wise friend. Similarly, we all experience some measure of darkness as we age and friends are lost either by death, relocation, or reduced communication. Life takes its toll not only physically but also socially as people's perspectives are restricted by the demands of life.

Further, there is an increasing recognition of the loss of self, as Nouwen and Gaffney note.[2] This is particularly felt in the aging process, where the good years all seem to exist in the past. The inner dialogue of "I used to be a somebody. People knew my name. I was respected and had power over others" gets louder. We tell ourselves, "I was strong and independent and was able to do what I wanted and go wherever I desired. But now I am weak. I can't remember things; I am told what to do, what to eat, where to sit and even when to go to bed." The deterioration in my father's health was a vivid picture of this reality. He had been a man of excellent fortitude well into his eighties. He was a great walker, having walked across England numerous times and also around the coasts of Ireland. His plunge into poor health was a massive shock as he had never physically suffered as much as a headache. He first lost his hearing, making communication challenging, followed by a loss of balance due to a series of mini-strokes impeding his walking. Cancer of the esophagus then appeared, which ultimately affected his vocal cords, negating his beautiful Belfast accent, and then proceeded to impact his sight, causing double vision. His eating and swallowing became demanding as the cancerous tumor continued to grow, restricting the size of his esophagus. He muttered to me one time after a slow breakfast, "Son, getting old is not for wimps! I can't hear! I can't see! I can't talk! I can't walk, and I can barely eat!" In that moment he mustered a degree of humor but in reality his loss of self was a painful journey into the unknown. He experienced all the isolation, desolation, and loss of self as his identity shrank from a global traveler to a weary chair- and apartment-bound solitary man.

My father's story emphasizes the reality that the experience of diminishment is a singular path. The value of family and a larger community is greatly helpful in assuaging the intensity of the descent but the journey remains a solo one. No one else experiences our walk as we do. It is a solitary descent

---

2. Ibid., 39.

into unknown country. C. S. Lewis utters this point when reflecting on the painful death of his wife from cancer after only a few years of marriage:

> You can't really share someone else's weakness, or fear or pain. What you feel may be bad. It might conceivably be as bad as what the other felt, though I should distrust anyone who claimed that it was. But it would still be quite different. . . . We both knew this. I had my miseries, not hers; she had hers, not mine. The end of hers would be the coming-of-age of mine.[3]

As the apostle Paul enjoins, "We must work out our own salvation with fear and trembling" (Phil 2:12), and this includes the descent of diminishment. As much as a spouse or friend, a mother or father, a sister or brother cares, the path one ultimately walks needs to be figured out alone.

OPPORTUNITIES OF DIMINISHMENT

If we accept our reality of diminishment over time there is a surprising liberation that leads us into a place of strength. It is not all desolation; there is also the experience of consolation. For example, seniors who enter into their retirement years often experience an increasing sense of rest and time to enjoy a new stage of life. This derives from a schedule with more space for spontaneity and enjoyment in the present moment. There is also more room for listening, spending time with others, and making a difference to the broader community through acts of service. We have seniors in our own faith community who offer service in ordinary time in exceedingly different ways: some prepare and serve meals for our church luncheons, others give their time in the maintenance of our aging building, and others call and visit the sick who are isolated in apartment towers. These various forms of service flow from the acceptance of a new season of life that is free of competition and the attempts to impress others through achievement. They come with a spirit of equanimity that says, "This is who I am and what I am able to do and I am okay with that." Such a humble and authentic spirit helps to build a community of service and love and also frees the individual to enjoy the immediate possibilities that life continues to offer.

Strength also is known as we recognize that while there is physical decline there may be great spiritual fecundity during the same period of time. The apostle Paul offers this perspective when he affirms,

---

3. Lewis, *Grief Observed*, 14–15.

LIGHT WITHIN THE STRUGGLE OF DIMINISHMENT

> So we do not lose heart. Even though our outer nature is wasting away, our inner nature is being renewed day by day. For this slight momentary affliction is preparing us for an eternal weight of glory beyond all measure, because we look not at what can be seen but at what cannot be seen; for what can be seen is temporary, but what cannot be seen is eternal. (2 Cor 4:16–18)

In another place he declares in his latter years, "I have fought the good fight, I have finished the race, I have kept the faith. From now on there is reserved for me the crown of righteousness, which the Lord, the righteous judge, will give to me on that day" (2 Tim 4:7–8). Such statements hold out the power of hope in Paul's life—and for the life of every person who follows Jesus through the death barrier—in the wake of Christ's resurrection. Hope is a dynamic force that empowers people to push ahead and to receive the *kairos* opportunities even within the path of diminishment. We acknowledge that certain patterns have to be changed as a result of our inevitable decline, but new vistas await that can be explored and enjoyed within life's new season. For example, as I observed the young people of our faith community planning a football tournament following our community lunch, I was struck by my new place in life. In the past I would have been all over such an event because of my years of playing on high school football teams and my general enjoyment of sports. However, due to Father Time, I now choose the sidelines to watch and cheer, safely protecting my knees and ligaments, so I can continue other interests like scuba diving! I will not be running full steam on a fly pattern to catch a soaring spiral but will be spending time with parishioners in conversation and good-natured critique of the game. I am hoping this alternative approach of enjoying the match will bear fruit for all as we cheer on the brave football players.

A third component within this season of change is the opportunity to embrace grace. So much of our life is spent in achieving and seeking more—more money, power, prestige, education, exotic travel.[4] With life's new rhythm we can begin to let go and simply receive the gifts that come to us. We think of the words of Aldous Huxley spoken to his dying wife: "Let go, let go . . . go forward into the light. Let yourself be carried into the light. No memories, no regrets, no looking backwards, no apprehensive thoughts about your own or anyone else's future. Only light. Only this pure being, this love, this joy."[5] Such a spirit of letting go happens as we accept

---

4. See Heschel, *Sabbath*, on "the acquisitive nature of contemporary society."
5. Huxley, *This Timeless Moment*, 28.

Part II — The Practice of Listening

the grace that Abba freely gives us—which we know we do not deserve and cannot demand—flowing from the limitless source of his love. It seems to take many years to realize that ultimately it is not a question of work, but of grace. The older folk who are closer to eternity seem to have a stronger grasp of this truth than those who are still in the years of power. The perception of this reality arrives at different times but the important point is that it arrives.

With my father and his long-standing Irish Protestant work ethic, the paradigm of works was deeply entrenched. He was a good man, an outstanding mate, as his Northern Ireland British roots encouraged. He worked hard with his brother Tom as co-owners of a body shop in Belfast (with the slogan "You bend it, we mend it") for about ten years and then left to join the thousands of Irish who immigrated to Canada in the early 1950s, seeking both adventure and new opportunities. Arriving in his adopted country, he learned, as all immigrants do, that life is challenging in a new land. He worked two jobs for a decade, as a body worker in Bealer's garage in Toronto and also as a night cleaner in Philip's Electronics in Leaside, before "getting on the pig's back" (as the Irish muse) with a career job at the Board of Education, first as a cleaner and later as a stationary engineer. All of his life he worked hard and it served him well, so it is not surprising he found the subject of pure grace a conundrum. He used to say, "Your mother has a simple faith. She simply accepts what the Scriptures teach. For me I just don't know . . ." Work made sense, even on faith matters; grace, on the other hand, had a sense of unfairness that riled his "I've been through the war and survived" mentality and obfuscated the acceptance of something free with little effort apparently required.

Fast-forwarding to his last days in the hospice, I visited him daily and one afternoon I asked him, "Dad, what are you thinking about all day?" He responded, "Mostly regrets," to which I naively retorted, "Dad, you don't want to go there. Think about your hope!" However, in those remaining hours his answer made more sense, with his approach to life and his high value of treating people in a certain way. His health failed rapidly after that visit. His pain increased and higher doses of medication were administered, which made him sleepy and restless. To my surprise, during one of my visits he suddenly leaned forward and blurted out the words, "Have mercy! Have mercy! Have mercy!" It was at that point I knew my father was ready to sail off to the distant shore, for he had accepted the free grace and mercy of his loving Abba. "Good for you, Dad! Good for you!," I whispered, and I sat there resting my hand on his. I saw the invitation clearly "to unfold our clenched fists and open our hands towards God," and in that act receive the grace that God has desired to give us throughout our life journey.[6] The writer of James reassures us: "Or do you suppose that it is for nothing that the scripture says, 'God yearns jealously for the spirit that he has made to dwell in us'? But he gives all the more grace; therefore it says, 'God opposes the proud, but gives grace to the humble'" (4:5–6).

LISTENING WITHIN DIMINISHMENT

The first step in listening begins with the acceptance of the natural rhythms of life, which includes the reality of diminishment. We see this attitude in the apostle Paul when he acknowledges that he has learned the ability of being content in all circumstances, whether in abundance or times of scarcity (Phil 4:11). In another letter he lists all of the ways that he has experienced challenges and hardship in his travels, fulfilling his vocation: "in danger from rivers, danger from bandits, danger from my own people, danger from Gentiles, danger in the city, danger in the wilderness, danger at sea, danger from false brothers and sisters; in toil and hardships, through many a sleepless night, hungry and thirsty, often without food, cold and naked" (2 Cor 11: 26–27). However, throughout it all he perseveres in his faith. The key is to acknowledge that the rhythm of growth and decline is intrinsic to the human condition. It is not just a trial to endure; rather, decline is endemic to the current of life that carries us all along. The reality of its power faces everyone sooner or later. The question is, how do we respond to it? Do we resist it in anger or blame, sadness or cynicism, denial or stoicism—or can we receive it as a dimension of the warp and woof of life's stream? Ronald Rolheiser encourages us with the latter, exhorting:

> Don't mummify: Let go, so as not to be pushed! Accept daily deaths. Do not hold on to life as possession. Possessiveness kills enjoyment. Let go of life gracefully. The greatest strength of life is the power to resign it. Death-corruption-resurrection, that is the true rhythm. Keep in mind that it is difficult to distinguish a moment of dying from a moment of birth.[7]

---

6. Nouwen, *With Open Hands*, 3–4.
7. Rolheiser, *Forgotten Among the Lilies*, 314.

Part II—The Practice of Listening

Second, listening occurs as we claim the joy that rises up within the cycle of diminishment. Moments of beauty serendipitously occur all along the way even during times of sickness or loss. During Jesus' last earthly days as he enjoys a meal at the house of Simon the leper, a woman approaches and anoints his head with an expensive perfume of alabaster. Others roundly critique the woman for her lavish act, but Jesus commends her and receives the gift as a beautiful sign of love (Mark 14:3–9). We also see Jesus celebrating a final meal with his disciples on the very night that he is to be betrayed (Luke 22:15–18). He is able to receive and celebrate the beautiful moments even as he moves towards the pain and suffering of the cross. Life presents its loveliness even during the downward trajectory of diminishment. In Marilynne Robinson's novel *Lila*, the aging minister draws together the simultaneous themes of pain and joy:

> Life on earth is difficult and grave and marvellous. Our experience is fragmentary. Its parts don't add up. They don't even belong in the same calculation. Sometimes it is hard to believe they are all parts of one thing . . . joy can be joy and sorrow can be sorrow with neither of them casting either light or shadow on the other."[8]

The key in receiving and living with this tension is not to be blinded by life's pain to such a degree that the resurrection joy is lost.[9]

Third, *kairos* moments continue to be revealed throughout the life journey—if we are paying close attention—and these points in time often unveil God's presence. A retired man in our church was speaking to me recently about the joys of his family though he was widowed in the last year. He shared that he has nine grandchildren and twelve great grandchildren and recently travelled to England to see them. He exclaimed to me, "I met them all, except for three of my great grandchildren, and now those three are unhappy and want me to return so I can meet them!" The trip to see his family became a joyful *kairos* encounter even though he carries grief over his wife's recent passing. Can we live open to the *kairos* possibility during our times of loss? In Roderick's work *Beloved* Henri Nouwen comments on an individual's response to a serious leg injury: the person may groan and say, "My career is over!," or have the insight to boldly assert, "I am receiving

---

8. Robinson, Marilynne. *Lila*, 223.

9. van Breemen, *The God Who Won't Let Go*, 149. Van Breemen acknowledges this idea from Mother Teresa who once said, "Nothing would ever fill us with so much sadness that it could make us forget the joy of the risen Lord."

Light within the Struggle of Diminishment

a new vocation."[10] The response is dependent on how open one is to receive something new from Abba. Likewise, joy bubbles up even in the midst of pain, sorrow, and loss when we are able to put on the wide-angle lens and see all that is offered.

Fourth, the invitation is to keep listening for the voice of Abba all along the way but especially in times of dislocation. Catherine Doherty tells us in her book *Poustinia* that her sickbed became an awakened place of prayer as she entered into the needs, cries, and pains of the other patients in the hospital.[11] Conversely, we often attempt to locate God in places of comfort; it may be better to look intently for him during our times of need, loss, and poverty. Doherty muses on this point, saying,

> I see Christ in poverty. He is most comfortable in poor places. He likes uncomfortable chairs; he likes to sleep on the floor . . . God is happy in simplicity and in poverty, especially poverty of spirit. A goal to strive for is to arrive at the point where 'the need to have becomes the need not to have.'[12]

Perhaps the Beatitudes provide the way for our faith journey, as they both begin and end with the spiritual fruitfulness of poverty:

> Blessed are the poor in spirit, for theirs is the kingdom of heaven. Blessed are those who mourn, for they will be comforted. (Matt 5:3–4)

> Blessed are those who are persecuted for righteousness' sake, for theirs is the kingdom of heaven. Blessed are you when people revile you and utter all kinds of evil against you falsely on my account. Rejoice and be glad, for your reward is great in heaven. (5:10–12)

When we are on the downward way the divine light is most intense, so let us keep our eyes and ears attuned to the gentle voice of Abba in such troubled times.

We are invited to see that diminishment is not a tragic end but a necessary piece in one's process of transformation. As the lapping waves soften the sharp edges of the shoreline, so Abba's transforming grace remakes us into the likeness of Jesus. In his masterpiece *The Divine Milieu*, Teilhard de Chardin speaks of the powerful work of diminution in the words of a

---

10. Roderick, *Beloved*, 37.
11. Doherty, *Poustinia*, 166–72.
12. Ibid., 81.

prayer. May his thoughts open up vistas of understanding as we listen for Abba's voice in life's darkest moments:

> Grant . . . that I may recognize you under the dark species of each alien or hostile force that seems bent upon destroying or uprooting me. When the signs of age begin to mark my body (and still more when they touch my mind); when the ill that is to diminish me or carry me off strikes from without or is born within me; when the painful moment comes in which I suddenly awaken to the fact that I am ill or growing old; and above all at that last moment when I feel I am losing hold of myself and am absolutely passive within the hands of the great unknown forces that have formed me; in all those dark moments, O God, grant that I may understand that it is you (provided only my faith is strong enough) who are painfully parting the fibres of my being in order to penetrate to the very marrow of my substance and bear me away within yourself.[13]

---

13. Teilhard de Chardin, *The Divine Milieu*, 89–90.

Light within the Struggle of Diminishment

QUESTIONS FOR FURTHER REFLECTION

1. In what ways has the path of suffering revealed Abba's touch on your life?

2. Diminishment brings with it the experience of loss. Write in your journal the effects of the downward path that have impacted you to the greatest degree.

3. Opportunities also happen during these significant times of change. Share with a friend in your prayer or study group how diminishment has opened up new paths of exploration or self-discovery.

4. As you have finished reading this chapter consider the question, how has the Holy Spirit impressed his drawings on your spirit concerning your own experience of loss? Write a psalm using your reflections to help you articulate your interior thoughts and questions.

Chapter 12

Creating Space

As Old Testament stories go, the one of Jacob conniving his brother out of his inheritance, orchestrated by his own mother, is up there with the best of them. In it he deceives his elderly father by disguising himself as his brother Esau, and receives the blessing that comes with the inheritance of his father Isaac and Abraham before him. Esau is enraged and plans his revenge. Jacob hightails it out of Beersheba to get to his uncle's place in Haran with the ploy of finding an acceptable wife rather than one of the Canaanite women. He is aware that his deception has turned sour and might just cost him his life. Exhausted from his running and his fear, he falls asleep and dreams of a ladder reaching from the earth up to heaven with angels ascending and descending. Then the Lord appears standing beside him and announces that he will protect him as he travels and will bring him safely back to the land, and in doing this will ultimately bless all the nations of the earth through his offspring (Gen 27–28:15). When Jacob wakes up he bursts out with relief and gratitude, "Surely the Lord is in this place—and I did not know it! How awesome is this place! This is none other than the house of God, and this is the gate of heaven" (28:16–17).

The hinge in this wonderful story is the line, "Surely the Lord is in this place and I did not know it!" It is only now—through the revelation in the vision—that he realizes how God has been with him all along. As a response to this epiphany he builds a stone pillar and calls it Bethel, "the house of God," his meeting place with God (Gen 28:22), and promises to honor him with his life as he continues his journey forward to Haran and beyond.

As Jacob learned this truth, so we are invited to understand that Abba travels with us in all of our experiences. He is at our side in every place we find ourselves—not only in the church sanctuary during Sunday morning worship, but at every juncture of time and space. He is with me as I write this chapter in a coffee shop on the edge of Lake Ontario and he is with you wherever you are reading these words. We also are invited to cry out, "Surely the Lord is with me in this place!" and come to recognize and experience his presence as we live our ordinary and extraordinary days. There may have been times when we did not perceive this astounding truth, but here and now we are invited to awaken to the consoling presence of God in the everyday. It is to this insight of Jacob that we turn in both the claiming and creating of space as a way of hearing and experiencing the voice of Abba in our lives.

EMBRACING SPACE

As we consider the stories of the patriarchs in Old Testament history we hear the recurring theme of God's promise concerning the land. God first promised the land in his call to Abraham, saying, "Go from your country and your kindred and your father's house to the land that I will show you. I will make of you a great nation, and I will bless you, and make your name great, so that you will be a blessing" (Gen 12:1-2). To Abraham's son Isaac he repeated the promise: "Reside in this land as an alien, and I will be with you, and will bless you; for to you and to your descendants I will give all these lands, and I will fulfill the oath that I swore to your father Abraham" (26:3). Once again, in our present story we hear God's promise to the conniving Jacob: "I am the Lord, the God of Abraham your father and the God of Isaac; the land on which you lie I will give to you and to your offspring . . . and all the families of the earth shall be blessed in you and in your offspring" (28:13-14).

The promise of God was always rooted in the land. As one writer puts it, "[The land] is the tangible token of God's faithfulness, the concrete expression of the covenant relationship, and the goal of Israel's wandering where the people will find rest. . . . Thus the land becomes the touchstone for life or death; it is given out of God's free grace, but retained by means of obedience."[1] It was immediate, solid terra under foot—something to be felt, walked upon, seen, experienced with our five senses. It was not a vision of ethereal afterlife, but a concrete expression of Abba's love known in day-to-day living. Indeed, it seems that for the nation of Israel the afterlife was a land of shadows known as *Sheol*. As one Old Testament scholar explains, "But the thought of going to *Sheol* was no comfort to the good man. The gloomy associations of death hung over this abode; it was figured as a land of silence and forgetfulness; the warm and rich light of the upper-world was excluded from it."[2] It was not really until the time of Daniel that Israel embraced a clear understanding of resurrection to life (Dan 12:2). Hence, the focus for the early generations of Israel was upon God's blessing of life in the land, here and now. It was an appreciation of creation and specifically of God's gift of the land, where people experienced his blessings and heavenly touch.

Israel's experience of the land is echoed in Margaret Craven's description of the Tsawataineuk village of Kingcome in the wilds of British Columbia:

> The Indian knows his village and feels for his village as no white man for his country, his town, or even for his own bit of land. His village is not the strip of land four miles long and three miles wide that is his as long as the sun rises and the moon sets. The myths are the village and the winds and the rains. The river is the village, and the black and white killer whales that herd the fish to the end of the inlet the better to gobble them. The village is the salmon who comes up the river to spawn, the seal who follows the salmon and bites off his head, the bluejay whose name is like the sound he makes—"Kwiss-Kwiss." The village is the talking bird, the owl, who calls the name of the man who is going to die, and the little white speck that is the mountain goat on Whoop-Szo.[3]

For Jacob and for the Tsawataineuk people the land becomes a place of epiphany. God shows up in the created order through the actions of his created beings and objects, as the psalmists love to celebrate: "The heavens are telling the glory of God; and the firmament proclaims his handiwork. Day to day pours forth speech, and night to night declares knowledge" (Ps 19:1–2); "You stretch out the heavens like a tent, you set the beams of your chambers on the waters, you make the clouds your chariot, you

---

1. Janzen, "Land," 147.
2. Orr, "Immortality in the Old Testament," 254.
3. Craven, *Owl Called My Name*, 12.

ride on the wings of the wind, you make the winds your messengers, fire and flame your ministers" (104:2–4); "You cause the grass to grow for the cattle, and plants for people to use, to bring forth food from the earth, and wine to gladden the human heart, oil to make the face shine, and bread to strengthen the human heart." (104:14–15).

Now it is our turn to stay awake and be alert to how God breaks into our daily world. Too often we are overcome with distraction. The clamor of background noise deafens and hurry becomes the theme of our day as we rush from appointment to appointment, event to event. Our infatuation with entertainment (literally "something that stands in between"[4])—whether sports or television shows or surfing the Net—distances us from the core experience of living our real lives. Harmless and even helpful entertainment for the purpose of relaxation can easily become excessive and habitual, dulling our focus on substantive activities. Within this noisy world it is challenging to hear Abba's voice and to pay attention to the ways that his Spirit breaks through in the hours and minutes of our daily journey. A specific step we can take in embracing our space is to open up to God's movement toward us in the spaces of our lives. We are invited to look with awareness as we take our steps throughout the day. We are called to hear the words of Jesus, "Sufficient is the day" (Matt 6:34 KJV), and not spend our time burdened by thoughts beyond the present day—whether the past or the future. This is not a call to live careless, poorly planned lives, but an invitation to take stock of our day as it lies there before us and consciously enter into each event and encounter that our day holds and reveals. We need time for careful reflection, pausing to ask ourselves how God might show up in the events of our day so that we do not miss the surprising movements of the Spirit. We ask ourselves specific questions: What events are scheduled for me this day? What personal encounters am I anticipating? How can I be in tune with any unexpected gifts that may emerge? Am I receptive to the holy breaking into my life through the hours that this day unfolds? As we take this deliberate action of slowing down and intentionally receiving our day, we open up the possibility of catching the Spirit's wave which is sure to break into our present moment. We become more aware of the moments that bubble up from God's eternal presence and his constant yearning for us (Jas 4:5).

---

4. "to keep ('tain' from the Latin *tenere*) something in between ('enter')." See Nouwen, *Can You Drink the Cup?*, 94.

Part II—The Practice of Listening

CREATING SPACE

We not only embrace the space where God is; we may need to create space to recognize God's voice. Again, we acknowledge the theological point that God is near. Jacob wakes up from his vision and declares, "God was in this place and I did not know it!" It is this reality that becomes lost in the disorder of our lives. The challenge is not just one of more efficient scheduling but of having minds that are not cluttered. Too often we have little mental or emotional space left for God to show up. We are filled with such inner turmoil, distress, and busyness that there is little space for spiritual reception. There is too much internal static to tune into Abba's signals of love and consolation. It is like having a computer so full of data that it keeps crashing; too much extraneous material is filling up the storage space so that everything slows down, freezes, and eventually stops functioning. We need to do an internal cleanse or data dump so we have room to spiritually breathe, receive healthy input, and forge new paths.

We want to create new space for the fundamental work of spiritual growth—to provide room for the seed of faith to grow and bear fruit. If the seed has to compete with contrary forces of rocks, weeds, lack of rain, and unhealthy soil, it is difficult for the seed to grow (see Mark 4:1-20). So if the first step is decluttering our lives to enable hearing from Abba, then the second is to intentionally create space where spiritually energizing input is received. The apostle Paul encourages us to have our minds renewed in Christ (Col 3:2), and that means to open up our intellectual capacity to the enlivening presence and activity of God. We need to reflect on how and where we can create new opportunities for receiving energy from the Spirit of God. Paul speaks of the "sharing" or *koinōnia* of the faith (Phlm 6), referring to intentionally aligning our lives with the Spirit in his work of kingdom building. In the *koinōnia* of the Spirit we become partners with Christ in our fundamental vocation of becoming like him. This *koinōnia* takes shape by saying yes to the purposes of God in our choices rather than our self-serving desires and preferences. We make space for God as we allow him freedom to shape us into the instruments that most effectively resonate with his purposes to become a conduit of his grace (2 Cor 4:7).

This space we have created to hear from God often takes the form of either stillness or praise. Stillness allows for the gentle whispers of Abba's voice to be heard and puts a pause on our busyness. In stillness we listen for the quiet movement of the Spirit like gentle waves lapping on the beach. We slow down and receive the moment and God's presence in it. It is up to us to choose the actual method for creating these points of stillness, but it is most important that they take place to allow for spiritual flourishing.

A second way of creating space and hearing from Abba occurs through the action of praising him. Praise has the power to shape our minds, tempering our ego-driven desires and enabling us to be more receptive to his Spirit. In praise we center on him so that his will becomes more apparent. We learn to recognize his voice and that is half the battle. We, as his loved ones, learn to hear the voice of our lover, even as the prophet Zephaniah reminded the people of Israel centuries ago, "He will rejoice over you with gladness, he will renew you in his love; he will exult over you with loud singing as on a day of festival" (Zeph 3:17). As we recognize his voice in the way Jesus affirms, "I know my own and my own know me . . . they will listen to my voice" (John 10:14, 16), we naturally respond to his overtures and set our feet on the paths where he is leading. In both stillness and praise we are led into enlarged spaces and places for meaningful and purposeful living.

HEALING SPACE

It is in space that God brings healing. As the Israelites are about to enter the promised land, the Lord encourages Joshua to lead them, saying, "Now proceed to cross the Jordan, you and all this people, into the land that I am giving to them, to the Israelites. Every place that the sole of your foot will tread upon I have given to you, as I promised to Moses" (Josh 1:2-3). The land as space becomes the place of *shalom*, bringing a peace encompassing health, abundance, and fullness of life for both the Israelites and for us. It speaks of both external and internal peace, a place where we have room to grow and cultivate our giftedness and also a peace within that fosters our relationship with God and his creation. Jesus alludes to this internal *shalom* when he stands up at the festival of Sukkot and invites people to receive from God the river of life that bubbles up through him bringing joy and abundance (John 7:37-39). Thus, *shalom* is God's gift to us in the here and now, which is realized interiorly but is lived out in the space that we occupy as we stay connected to Jesus in an intentional and passionate manner.

As we embrace this dynamic space, it becomes a place to celebrate and to deepen our relationship with Abba. A spiritual aid that assists us in this direction is the gift of the Sabbath. The Sabbath becomes a celebration in time of our relationship with God in the land. It is a meeting place between time and space where interior and exterior needs are met and growth is nourished. Abraham Heschel calls the Sabbath "a palace in time" given to us for the bringing and celebration of life. He explains, "The seventh day is a palace in time which we build. It is made of soul, of joy and reticence. In its atmosphere, a discipline is a reminder of adjacency to eternity."[5] He understands the rhythm of life in a pattern designed by God: "Six days a week we wrestle with the world, wringing profit from the earth; on the Sabbath we especially care for the seed of eternity planted in the soul. The world has our hands, but our soul belongs to Someone Else."[6]

In light of our propensity to busyness there is a need to hear the ongoing value the Scriptures claim for the role of the Sabbath. We begin with the pivotal creation text that declares, "And on the seventh day God finished the work that he had done, and he rested on the seventh day from all the work that he had done. So God blessed the seventh day and hallowed it, because on it God rested from all the work that he had done in creation" (Gen 2:2–3). What God modeled he expects of his people, as found in the first command of the Decalogue:

> Remember the sabbath day, and keep it holy. For in six days you shall labour and do all your work. But the seventh day is a sabbath to the Lord your God; you shall not do any work. . . . For in six days the Lord made heaven and earth, the sea, and all that is in them, but rested on the seventh day; therefore the Lord blessed the seventh day and consecrated it. (Exod 20:8–11)

The Sabbath provides a break from constant work and becomes a day "unto the Lord," offering a place for spiritual refreshment and worship to God. As a creation mandate the Sabbath traverses time, becoming an invitation to break free from the drivenness of our utilitarian culture that values consumption and materialism at the expense of rest and re-creation.

In the Deuteronomic presentation of the Decalogue an equally important principle for keeping the Sabbath is given: the liberation of those who are in bondage. We hear the text supporting this foundational theme:

> Observe the sabbath day and keep it holy, as the Lord your God commanded you . . . you shall not do any work—you, or your son or your daughter, or your male or female slave, . . . or the resident alien in your towns, so that your male and female slave may rest as well as you. Remember that you were a slave in the land of Egypt, and the Lord your God brought you out from there with a mighty

---

5. Heschel, *Sabbath*, 14–15.
6. Heschel, *I Asked for Wonder*, 34.

hand and an outstretched arm; therefore the Lord your God commanded you to keep the sabbath day. (Deut 5:12–15)

In this rendition of the command the creation mandate is replaced with a liberation injunction that provides further support for keeping the Sabbath—the command to work for liberation, justice, and freedom for all disempowered peoples. The Sabbath principle helps to energize us for the task of bringing liberation for marginalized groups.[7]

In the New Testament we hear the words of Jesus urging us to recognize the permanent role that the Sabbath plays. In one story we read that his disciples were being criticized for plucking ears of corn on the Sabbath because they were hungry. Jesus defends their actions by citing how David and his companions entered the house of God and ate the bread of the presence, and then he delivers the dictum, "The sabbath was made for humankind, and not humankind for the sabbath; so the Son of Man is lord even of the sabbath" (Mark 2:23–28; see also Matt 12:1–8). Jesus does not argue that Sabbath keeping no longer applies; rather he contends that the leaders of the day are misapplying the principle so that its essential purpose of giving nourishment for humankind is lost. The Sabbath is meant to support our experience of *shalom*, not take it away through legalistic rules. It provides us with a sense of space so that we do not become enslaved to a frenetic culture that focuses primarily on having and doing. We are invited to celebrate "being"—living integrated lives of body, mind, and spirit, leading us into fullness of life and glorifying our Heavenly Father.

One of the ways that the Sabbath brings healing is through the sense of stability that it establishes. The Sabbath creates a model of work and rest, keeping us grounded; we work for six days and then have a day to rest from our labor. To use a visual example, our lives are no longer represented by a dotted line symbolizing ceaseless work but as a circle encompassing both work and rest. The circle model allows us to plumb the possibilities of the place that we inhabit. It returns us to our point of contact to explore options, variations, and development. It is similar to the sonata form in music, where both recapitulation and embellishment are built into the structure, creating new expressions of musical life. The Sabbath invites us to dig deep into our allotted space and fill it with creative vibrancy, to claim our home space and make it a life affirming reality that embodies both *shalom* and creative living. In *Free Play: Improvisation In Life and Art*, Stephen Nachmanovitch suggests,

---

7. See also Amos 8:4–6 and Isa 56:4–6 for Sabbath keeping related to issues of justice.

Part II—The Practice of Listening

> Perhaps the most radical sociopolitical invention of the past four thousand years was the sabbath. The practice of the sabbath . . . recognizes that we need space and time reserved from the rushing and pressures of everyday life, reserved for going inside ourselves, for rest, review, and revelation.[8]

He speaks of Walt Whitman's celebration of "the value of loafing," where one is alert to the possibilities of the moment and has creative space to explore the unexpected happenings that emerge when both space and time are allowed to fuel rather than to drive us.[9]

The Sabbath invites us to discover Abba's rhythm in our own lives. In a spirit of repose each of us is able to ask the question, how does God reveal himself in the everyday? We want to learn God's ways of engaging with us personally and listen for his voice along the lines that he chooses. Marva Dawn provides possible modern paths for keeping the Sabbath. She uses the word "feasting" as a way of capturing relaxed sabbath time and space instead of our propensity to hurry and rush from event to event. Her suggestions include feasting with music, feasting with beauty, feasting with food, feasting with affection, feasting and festival.[10] In this list we are invited to explore the possibilities of music, beauty, food, hospitality, and seasonal celebrations as ways of going deeper with God—to provide opportunity to sit with these expressions and explore their subtleties and colors. These expressions may resonate with us at some level, some more than others. Along with Dawn's illustrative suggestions, we have also considered the roles of worship, creation, word, prayer, silence, solitude, and community—all elements that could become part of our own Sabbath keeping. These and many others are potential paths of discovery in knowing and hearing Abba's whisper through our journey in time and space. When it comes to healing space we all have to do our own work so that we find the places of contact—the "thin places" of Celtic mysticism where heaven and earth come together and almost touch—with the eternal movements of our loving God.[11]

---

8. Nachmanovitch, *Free Play*, 155.
9. Ibid., 154. Albeit, Whitman is not referring to the Sabbath!
10. Dawn, *Keeping the Sabbath Wholly*, 166–202.
11. See Pemberton, *Soulfaring*, 18.

Creating Space

LISTENING SPACE

Space invites us to discover God in a specific place even as Jacob proclaimed, "God was in this place and I did not know it!" Every place on earth has the potential of becoming a sacred place. Can we open our eyes to examine the reality that shines before us? It is not about a consideration of abstract theological or philosophical ideas but about penetrating the essence of what really exists in the place where we are. It is the ability to free the child in each one of us, to see what we see and enjoy the moment that contains our existence. We are amazed when we see our young grandchildren play with simple things like small colourful wooden blocks that they mix and match, pile up and knock over, or arrange in interesting formations. They look at them, move them, feel them, even taste them!—all as a way of exploring the possibilities they offer. They are contented to fill the space they occupy and not complain about a space they do not have. Jesus invites us to become like them; indeed, he challenges us saying that without such a childlike spirit we will never enter the kingdom of heaven (Matt 18:1–5). Surely this injunction invites us to slow down—humble ourselves—so that the deep memories of childlikeness rise up through the hard layers reason, utility, pride, and consumption have formed. The childlike spirit embraces space as a friend to be enjoyed and not simply used; we receive what is offered and wait for what it is not yet ready to yield. When we live in our space we are able to receive the truth it contains and this opens us to hearing the voice of God.

Listening for Abba's voice happens as we claim our home space. When we neglect our place by constant movement and anxiety or fill it with so much stuff that it can hardly breathe, we fall into the traps of distraction and clutter that mask his whispers. Such attitudes and practices weaken the power of land and space and the benefits they engender for spiritual life. We lose touch with our place and our soul withers as a seed without water and sunshine. Good friends of mine lived in the Canadian Arctic for eight years and they have seen the devastation of indigenous peoples removed from the land and forced to live in the government-initiated "box towns." The result has been a gradual diminishment of a people's soul as they lose touch with the water, the ice, the bear, and the seal. In many ways a similar denuding of spirit happens to us when we fail to make a connection with our land and space. We lose touch with the place of epiphany as we are always hovering over our space instead of entering it. Jesus, the Lord of the earth, concerned himself with a small bit of land named Galilee and Judea;

he never travelled across the continents or sailed even the Mediterranean. He chose to know one place deeply to the benefit of the earth and all of its peoples. We can learn from his modeling as we go deeper in the space where he has placed us. We can know our own space—experience it—go deeper where we are, and listen for Abba's voice.

Practically, this focus means living deeply in our place and time under the sun. We take our place and God's movements in it seriously. A preacher once described Christian discipleship in his country as being "a hundred miles wide and a foot deep," by which he meant individuals used an abundance of Christian jargon in their day-to-day living but did not go deep in their relationship with God. It was all surface, and depth connections had not been plumbed because of a lack of commitment and perseverance. We are called to embrace our vocations and to know our piece of terra firma as a way of knowing the larger world. When we experience the spiritual epiphany emanating in "this place," "this family," "this community," we begin to embrace the vastness of Abba's possibilities that are revealed in a single grain of sand.

In this regard, we continue to learn from members of our church congregation who live in the heart of Weston. They do not have the financial resources to travel abroad or explore the greater boundaries of Canada. Yet, they live deeply in the church community by fostering relationships with friends in the places where they find themselves. They call each other daily and connect to tell stories, share prayer requests, eat meals, and worship in song and praise. They walk the streets, know their neighbors, talk and aid the street people, visit the local coffee shops, and buy local. In these ways they journey deep into the community's soul, living full lives that reverberate with the place and its people. As they do so they hear the whispers of Abba that rise up and they become a priestly presence demonstrating his love on the streets and corners of old Weston town.

We are also called to listen for Abba's voice in our familiar places, not neglecting them in search of more glamorous and distant locales. May we proceed slowly and pause long enough over our land so that the epiphanies of spirit may be seen and our souls cry out with Jacob, "Surely the Lord was in this place. . . . How awesome is this place!"

CREATING SPACE

QUESTIONS FOR REFLECTION

1. In what ways do you embrace or resist the space that you find yourself in? If you embrace your space list some of the ways that help you do this. If you are resisting what are the reasons for doing so?

2. Often we feel that are minds are too cluttered and that we have no mental or emotional space left to live creative lives. Can you identify steps to help declutter your life and provide more space to hear God's voice?

3. We have drawn attention to the role that Sabbath keeping can play in living healthy lives. What modern forms of keeping Sabbath sustain and give you rest amidst the challenges of life?

4. Describe the ways that place brings fecundity to your spiritual journey. Write a psalm of thanks for the places where Abba has revealed himself in your life—perhaps a cottage, a camp, a favorite hiking spot, a room of your own, or a nook in a library.

Chapter 13

Snail-Pace Discipleship

ONE OF MY FAVORITE environs for scuba diving is the Pacific Northwest. Everything is huge—whether it be the giant Pacific octopus (the largest octopus on the planet), sleek black and white orcas, or the lion's mane jellyfish. Even some of the smaller creatures such as plumose anemones or sea stars are still massive within their own species! Some race along, like the bulky sea lion that almost ran me over as I meandered through a kelp bed. Others move slowly, like a hungry sunflower star with as many as twenty arms zeroing in on an unsuspecting sea urchin. The sunflower stars are able to race along at a rapid seven feet a minute (which in the mollusk world is light speed), whereas a slug, more glamorously known as a nudibranch, moves at the velocity of the proverbial snail! In the underwater world these creatures are exceedingly colorful and beautiful as an impressionist Monet, but they are still as slow as a sloth.

In many ways our Christian discipleship moves "at a snail's pace" as Teresa of Avila once mused, and resembles the path of our beautiful but ponderous underwater friends.[1] The journey of faith requires us to take off the "old clothes" of our former nature, including impurity, evil desires, greed, anger, wrath, malice, and abusive language (Col 3:5, 8), and put on the "new clothes" of compassion, kindness, humility, meekness, patience, forgiveness, and love (Col 3:12–14). The apostle Paul emphasizes that this "putting off" and "putting on" is a process that needs to be constantly en-

---

1. Teresa of Avila, *Interior Castle*, 65.

gaged in an intentional manner. The old order with its old practices will continue to press in on us even as we put on the new clothes of Christ. If we become lazy, distracted, or flirt with evil, the old self will rise up and catch us in an unguarded state. Hence, there is the need for vigilance and the putting on of the new mind through saturation in the Scriptures with conscious praise of God (Col 3:16–17). A constant putting on of Jesus is required even as we wrestle with our old ways in a "three steps forward, two steps back" dance step. We are discouraged when we recognize our inadequacy and slow progress, but we must persevere and trust in the power of Abba to save us. We keep moving ahead in the spiritual battle through the workings of his energizing Holy Spirit (Eph 6:10–18). In this ongoing process of taking off and putting on, the gait of discipleship is painfully slow, but within this snail-like pace Abba's voice is discernible if we keep paying attention.

MESSY SPIRITUALITY

Life is messy and full of unexpected turns. A child needs teeth extractions; a friend is suddenly diagnosed with brain cancer; pink slips are unceremoniously handed out at the office; potential job opportunities fade away; life-long friends move to other parts of the country. Twists and turns increase our levels of anxiety, stress, and sadness. This is the nature of life—full of change and disruptions that compete with our desire to live comfortably and consistently. As a result, our spirituality becomes messy, as Mike Yaconelli describes.[2] We do not experience the beatific vision but live harried lives in a harried world. Yaconelli writes:

> The way of the spiritual life begins where we are now in the mess of our lives. Accepting the reality of our broken flawed lives is the beginning of spirituality, not because the spiritual life will remove our flaws but because we let go of seeking perfection and, instead, seek God, the One who is present in the tangled-ness of our lives. Spirituality is not about being fixed, it is about God being present in the mess of our unfixedness.[3]

In our messiness we often keep opening ourselves to the presence of God, but in spite of our best intentions, hurdles trip us up. What are these hurdles?

---

2. Yaconelli, *Messy Spirituality*, 15.
3. Ibid., 6.

Part II — The Practice of Listening

While the challenges are different for everyone, the core of the problem is fear. We live with a fear-shaped hole in our hearts. It seems Jesus understood our propensity to fear; the most prolific command in Scripture is "Do not be afraid." It is spoken to Zechariah, the priest serving in the temple (Luke 1:13); to Mary by Gabriel announcing her favor with God (Luke 1:30); to the shepherds watching their sheep at night (Luke 2:10); to Joseph anxious about his future with his pregnant fiancé (Matt 1:20); by Jesus calming his frightened disciples in a storm (Mark 6:50). We need to hear the words "Do not be afraid" because we carry so much fear within ourselves.

We try to cover up this fear hole in various ways. Busyness is one of them. We stay on the move, providing no time or space to think deeply. We run, and in our running try to escape the concerns that rise up if we pause to rest; so we keep running. Endless activity keeps the shadows from closing in. Desire or avarice is another approach to assuage our anxiety. We buy things; we fill up our homes with stuff so that hardly an empty space remains. "More, more, more" is the refrain our world sings with its attempt to mask fear. Control is another common tendency. We look for order, routine, comfort, and zero surprises. If we keep "all our ducks in a row" then fear cannot break in. Unfortunately, control is difficult to maintain as the vicissitudes of life mock our feeble attempts. Isolation is another road we travel in an attempt to withdraw from the craziness of life. We try to reduce contact with all but a select few in order to keep peace of mind, but soon learn that "no man is an island." Even in our places of retreat the worries of life surreptitiously crawl over the barriers we have erected. Last of all, we try to outperform everyone else so that a feeling of accomplishment and superiority calms the voices of competition and comparison. We say to ourselves, "I am the best at what I do," "My place is secure," and "I cannot be replaced!"—all ways of coping with the underlying fear that "I will lose my place" and "I need to keep up the facade of managing the balls in the air." Deep down we know the crash is coming and great will be its fall. This is the messy fearful way of living.

My own best attempts for spiritual formation sometimes resemble my home office, where papers and books are scattered on the floor, clothes are strewn, marked papers sit bundled in one pile beside the unmarked ones loosely scattered on the floor—not to mention the dive gear that has not quite reached the dive room in the basement! All of this bemuses my grandchildren, who exclaim over my "messy" office.

OUR PATIENT GOD

The good news is that Abba's response to our messiness is one of patience and grace. Our God knows all about our weakness and cares for us as a loving father or mother. As the longing father receives his prodigal son, so Abba waits for us and receives us with open arms when we wake up and come to our senses (Luke 15:17–24). God's response is one of compassion and generosity as he pours out his love to a heart that turns toward its creator. The description of Abba by the authors of *Compassion* is perceptive in its tenderness:

> The God-with-us is a close God, a God whom we call our refuge, our stronghold, our wisdom, and even, more intimately, our helper, our shepherd, our love.... The truly good news is that God is not a distant God, a God to be feared and avoided, a God of revenge, but a God who is moved by our pains and participates in the fullness of the human struggle.[4]

God is absolutely in solidarity with us as we live through the pains of life and struggle to come to spiritual maturity. He knows the trials we experience and the enemy we face, as his son Jesus Christ himself experienced the challenges common to the human condition (Heb 4:15). Abba knows our weakness from the inside out and is full of love and compassion for us even as we swing wildly in our pain, confusion, and frustration.

The Gospel of Matthew records a parable not found in the other Gospels emphasizing the quality of patience that God has toward us. It tells the story of a farmer who sows good seed on his land but while he sleeps an enemy comes and sows weeds (darnel) throughout the same field. The field workers wonder, "Shall we pull out the weeds mixed in with the wheat?" The owner wisely insists that to protect the wheat they must allow both the wheat and the weeds to grow. At the future harvest the needed separation will take place (Matt 13:24–30). The parable can be understood on a variety of levels, including "Jesus' own ministry, the life of the church, and the future judgment at the end of the world."[5] However, the parable is also instructive for the personal journey of faith. God has planted the good seed of life into our hearts through his grace and the seed is slowly maturing as all seeds do. The "enemy" personified in the Evil One, and our own proclivity to attachment—pleasure, desire, control, power, or pride—resists the seed's growth

---

4. McNeill et al., *Compassion*, 15, 18.
5. Long, *Matthew*, 151.

and produces weeds instead. The beauty of the parable is seen in the patience and grace of the farmer/owner. He allows the fragile seed to continue maturing in spite of its entanglement with the weeds, knowing that extraction at this point will harm its life. Similarly, God patiently waits on us as we struggle with our addictions and attachments in our spiritual adolescence, knowing that in time the good fruit will be born and the chaff will be blown away. In our haste we desire spiritual maturity instantly, but God in his patience realizes that time, experience, and a host of spiritual graces are necessary for the seed to make the long journey to fullness and fruitfulness.

We are called by the apostle Paul "God's work" which "he created" (Eph 2:10)—"God's workmanship" (NIV) or "God's work of art" (Jerusalem Bible) or "God's handiwork" (New English Bible). These translations remind us that we are a piece of art crafted by the Creator of the universe and that this process is not restricted to his work in the womb but to our entire process of becoming like his Son Jesus. This is a lifelong journey, and indeed, often gains momentum in the years of final descent—or ascent! In the Tyndale Chapel there are a series of fourteen marble carvings by the New York sculptor Donald De Lue depicting the Stations of the Cross. These carvings are placed into the sidewalls of the chapel, seven on each side, telling the story of Christ from his meeting with Pilate to his body being placed in the tomb. In all but three of the carvings women are situated in the background, expressing their deep emotional responses to the sight of Christ bearing the cross through the various scenes towards the tomb. The marble slabs received many blows by the artist, as he shaped and revealed the beauty that he had in mind. The result is a stunning collection that tells the story of Jesus and his sacrificial love as well as offering a journey in spiritual formation for all who attend to their beauty.

Likewise, we experience many blows thorough our life journey in becoming the unique piece of art that God is shaping. We do not understand the process. Every strike hurts, chunks are discarded that we are attached to, scenes are revealed that we never imagined, figures appear and become part of the story as complete surprises. However, there is also exquisite beauty as the story is told and the work of art takes its final form. I think of a lifelong friend who is dying from brain cancer—a traumatic time, but also a beautiful dance to behold as my friend draws closer to Abba through his last days. The final strokes of the Master are falling and the beauty comes into focus as the masterpiece is completed. Our artist God is a patient God who calls us to equally be forbearing even as we sometimes just see the messy discarded chips of the Sculptor at work.

GETTING STUCK AND UNSTUCK

The consequence of this painful process of spiritual formation is a journey of becoming stuck and unstuck in our movement towards Abba. We make great strides of turning things over to God, experiencing exquisite times of consolation, and then suddenly crash into a cement wall that stops our ascent and evokes the pain and confusion of spiritual desolation. Rather than climb the spiritual mountain we feel derailed, and either tumble down the mountain or get stuck on a ledge, unmoving and without hope. Such times are disconcerting and we contemplate giving up. Again, Yaconelli is most helpful as he advises,

> Getting stuck is a great moment, a summons, a call from within, the glorious music of disaffection and dissatisfaction with our current place in life. We get stuck when we want to change, but can't; when we want to stop destructive behaviour, but don't; when the tug-o-war between God's will and ours stands still and we can't move . . . Getting stuck . . . halts the momentum of our lives; we have no choice but to notice what is around us—and we end up searching for Jesus.[6]

From this point of view, getting stuck is not a spiritual disaster but a precursor for new life as we begin the process of considering optional routes to scale the mountain before us.

The film *The Imitation Game* instructs us in the experience of becoming stuck, telling the true story of Alan Turing, who was hired by the British to crack the Nazi communication code during the Second World War. As a young boy at boarding school Alan was harassed by older students and abused in various ways. Alan and his one friend, Christopher Morcom, become students of cryptology and write secret messages to each other, which ultimately fuels Alan's ability to break the Nazi code. Christopher recognizes his friend's giftedness, saying, "Sometimes it is the people no one imagines anything of who do the things that no one can imagine." Alan repeats this wonderful line later in life to one of the candidates when he is building the team to work on the Nazi code project, even while others

---

6. Yaconelli, *Messy Spirituality*, 105–6.

dismiss this person because she is a woman. Years later when Alan has fallen on hard times, the candidate, Joan, searches him out and encourages him with his own words, "Sometimes it is the people no one imagines anything of who do the things that no one can imagine."

So yes, we become spiritually stuck. We wonder if there is any spark left within us at all. Life seems sterile, frozen, and hopeless. The Deceiver whispers in our ear, "What is the point? Stop being a hypocrite! Simply give up on all of this God stuff." Yes, the temptations come fast and often, and our spiritual life seems to be at a dead end. How does Abba respond to us in these discombobulating stuck times when we wonder if our lives have amounted to anything? I believe he softly, lovingly, whispers our name and says, "Keep going. Keep trusting in me. Keep climbing the mountain. "I am with you and for you." "Sometimes it is the people no one imagines anything of who do the things that no one can imagine."

TAKING STOCK AND ALTERING COURSE

What then is our path forward? One suggestion is to take stock of our present situation—to re-evaluate our context by asking the questions, "Where, how, and in what specific ways am I stuck?" We need to be able to identify the blocks that are tripping us up and the issues that are preventing us from moving forward. Rationalizing away our problems keeps us from naming the real challenges we face and creating strategies to deal with them. For example, if I have a history of shouting and blowing up at others, perhaps the problem is my anger and not the behavior of those around me. If I am regularly comparing myself with colleagues and their success, perhaps the issue is my own avarice or insecurity. If I choose to constantly work and resist any down time, then perhaps the real issue at play is my desire to impress others with my importance rather than a heavy workload. It is important to name and own the ways that we are becoming stuck. Too often we accept debilitating issues because we are comfortable with the compensations—the high from the substance abuse, the emotional outburst that intimidates family members, the sad depressive state that controls others—more than the negative impact that our actions have on ourselves and others.

A second suggestion is simplification. Frequently, our lives are cluttered with extra activities that keep us in a state of perpetual motion but, ironically, stuck on a spiritual level. Thomas Kelly speaks of this tendency as both an internal and external busyness that keeps us distracted and spiritually frozen:

> We Western peoples are apt to think our great problems are external, environmental. We are not skilled in the inner life, where the real roots of our problem lie. . . . The outer distractions of our interests reflect an inner lack of integration of our own lives. We are trying to be several selves at once, without all our selves being organized by a single, mastering Life within us. Each of us tends to be, not a single self, but a whole committee of selves.[7]

Kelly encourages us to pursue an inner union with God so that integration of focus becomes our practice, simplifying our choices and maintaining the unifying presence of Abba. As we live from this center we continue an inner dialogue that helps us evaluate the options before us: "If I take on this responsibility will it deepen my relationship with God or become a distraction that creates distance?" "Will saying 'yes' to this administrative project create undo stress that leads to frustration?" "Does exploration of this opportunity (or promotion) aid in my core life work or side track me from it?" The encouragement is to seek greater clarity of our vision and responsibilities rather than obfuscation. Clarity happens as we stay true to our vocation, not lured by the voices of power, money, or fame that affirm one's ego at the expense of focus and creative work. An example of this approach is found in the acclaimed Canadian poet Margaret Avison, who consistently turned down upwardly mobile career opportunities so she could maintain her work and focus as a poet. She refused positions of advancement (and more pay) that would potentially complicate and interfere with her time to write. Avison modeled this interior dialogue that assists in keeping one straight about life's fundamental calling—to know Abba—and how it works itself out in constructive daily choices and decisions. Turning toward simplification and clarity propels us forward when we are stuck. Elucidating our choices provides a measure of traction to get the wheels moving, enabling an escape from moribund ruts.

Third, there is the invitation to make changes and alter course direction. Little changes are often more successful than huge ones. Flying to the moon involves more than lift off, a hard left or right, taking the capsule directly to our planetary companion; rather, it involves a continual sequencing of tiny adjustments for the spaceship to reach its desired goal. Or, closer to home, the Chi-Cheemaun ferry to Manitoulin Island requires time and small bursts of power to overcome backwards motion and gain forward momentum when leaving the dock in Tobermory. Similarly, if we

---

7. Kelly, *Testament of Devotion*, 91.

want to become spiritually unstuck we have to begin with tiny steps to get us going. The wisdom literature of Proverbs instructs us at this juncture, encouraging us to look to the ants and learn from the tiny creatures who work in small but powerful ways: "Go to the ant, you lazybones; consider its ways, and be wise" (6:6); "the ants are a people without strength, yet they provide their food in the summer" (30:25). The wisdom writer employs the ant as a model for taking small, intentional steps, leading one forward to the achievement of goals and desired outcomes. If the goal then is to become unstuck the following questions may be helpful: What tiny steps can we take to move forward? What changes can we initiate that create a bit of momentum? For example, in meditation, instead of beginning with long periods of quiet (i.e., thirty to sixty minutes), one begins in small ways (i.e., five minutes of quiet three times a week) to promote success. Identifying and implementing small changes into one's schedule engender degrees of movement that can be sustained and grow over time. Once again we are reminded of "seed power," as it has the space and time to take root and bring forth its harvest.

Fourth, we underline the importance of repetition in the establishment of a new routine and practice. Writers on the process of change remind us that a new habit needs to be repeated consistently and over time to establish it in one's daily routine. Brian Tracey makes this point:

> According to the experts, it takes about twenty-one days to form a habit pattern of medium complexity. By this, we mean simple habits such as getting up earlier at a specific hour, exercising each morning before you start out, listening to audio programs in your car, going to bed at a certain hour, being punctual for appointments, planning every day in advance.[8]

It is no different in establishing a new spiritual discipline. We need to start in small ways, take small steps, and practice it daily until it is established as part of our spiritual regime. Tracey emphasizes, "Never allow an exception to your new habit during the formative stages," affirming the point that repetition is required to build new choices into our lives.[9] Many of my students decide to spend thirty minutes with Abba first thing in the morning. Those that are successful harness the power of daily repetition (for twenty-one days), which builds the practice into their routine. If they start missing days the habit weakens and often fails. The good news is that "getting stuck is

---

8. Tracey, "Seven Steps to Developing a New Habit."
9. Ibid.

SNAIL-PACE DISCIPLESHIP

the prerequisite to getting unstuck," so with a measure of intentionality, new patterns can be formed, movement can be re-engaged, and spiritual freedom can replace the moribund patterns of old.[10]

HEARING ABBA IN SNAIL PACE DISCIPLESHIP

How do we hear Abba's voice during times of slow growth or no spiritual growth at all? The secret seems to be in the power of the fleeting glance towards Abba. Gerald May points this out in his book *The Awakened Heart*:

> The interior glance does not necessarily mean looking inward; it simply happens interiorly. It is a contemplative look Godward. It is an attitude of the heart leaning toward the truth of God's presence, or a flash of the mind opening to the remembrance of being in love. . . . Little interior glances are simple things; unadorned remembrances and noticings happening within the ordinary activities of our daily lives.[11]

As May suggests, all it takes is a furtive glance! In the midst of our pain or frozenness, God awaits the smallest glance, desire, or longing in his direction. May refers to this aspiration as a "homecoming" to God, a returning to our first love, the foundational desire for the Holy One.[12] The challenge is to be reminded of his loving presence even as we spiral downwards. Can we muster the strength to look his way during times of desolation—when we are in pain, when life seems flat, boring, and uninteresting? Are we able to return to Abba by way of the fleeting glance, reminding us of our true home and the One our heart deeply longs for?

Returning recognizes that we have been away. We have drifted by the current's pull toward other things, usually in the direction of our attachments. Lost in life's spinning motion, we look away from Abba instead of looking toward him. George Bernard Shaw, the great playwright, captures this reality of distraction in his play *Saint Joan*, portraying the Dauphin's response to Joan and her voices:

> "Oh, your voices, your voices," he said, "Why don't the voices come to me? I am king, not you."

---

10. Yaconelli, *Messy Spirituality*, 105.

11. May, *Awakened Heart*, 134. He acknowledges "the interior glance" is a phrase from Brother Lawrence, *Practice of the Presence of God*.

12. May, *Awakened Heart*, 7.

Part II—The Practice of Listening

> "They do come to you," said Joan, "But you do not hear them. You have not sat in the field in the evening listening for them. When the angelus rings you cross yourself and have done with it; but if you prayed from your heart, and listened to the thrilling of the bells in the air after they stop ringing, you would hear the voices as well as I do."[13]

As Joan entreats the king to look God's way, we are similarly invited to stop racing through life unaware of the divine presence and to glance in the direction of Abba as we engage our daily walk.

May also enjoins us to take little steps to prime the pump of looking toward God. These steps include the power of gathering with like-minded friends who seek to hear from Abba and staying in regular communication with them. The gathering for worship is important in remembering and hearing from God. We might want to "sprinkle our experience with physical reminders"[14] to help us recall our commitment to hear Abba, to help ourselves back to God by taking these tiny concrete steps that slow the casual drift away and return us in the direction towards Abba. The inward glance reminds us that life is more than simple existence and all of its demands. There is a greater arc holding the entire journey together through the seasons and filling the years, months, weeks, and days with a foundational direction toward our destiny of love. Turning our eyes toward Abba helps to sustain us during our snail pace discipleship, even as we learn that moving slowly offers many rewards on the path of openness and receptivity to divine love.

---

13. Barclay, *Good Tidings of Great Joy*, 45.
14 May, *Awakened Heart*, 142.

QUESTIONS FOR FURTHER REFLECTION

1. In what ways does your spiritual journey seem messy? Can you identify the reasons for the messiness and how you try to deal with it in every day life? How does knowing that Abba is a patient God encourage you as you attempt to sort things out with him?

2. Becoming stuck in one's spiritual formation is a common experience. Can you describe an experience of becoming spiritually stuck and unstuck and how it subsequently impacted your faith walk.

3. Making small adjustments seems to be a necessary part of the discipleship process. Write down in your journal some of the adjustments you have made and how they have aided your faith journey.

4. Does the term "snail-pace discipleship" seem to describe your journey with God? If so, write down some of the ways you have heard from Abba during your slow journey of faith. Exchange stories of your experience with a soul friend as a way of mutual encouragement.

Chapter 14

The Cry of Absence

THE FOUR DISTINCT SEASONS we enjoy in Toronto mirror the spiritual life running through its seasonal rhythm. There is the short spring season of sprouting life and rapid growth even as plants respond to the sunshine and spring showers. The explosion of greenery in the month of May turns bare streets into canvasses of green. Spiritually this awakening occurs as new believers drink from the springs of life and the spiritual world takes root. The spring flows into the summer and the foundations of one's spiritual life become strengthened through the Word, prayer, and participation in the faith community. Then fall comes, where life slows, allowing time for gentle change; the leaves are transformed into beautiful colors, slowly falling, revealing once again a bare landscape. This can be a time when one's experience of consolation is muted as we resist change and fail to recognize the beauty that the season holds. Finally, the winter season hits with both its snow-clad beauty and the harshness that the extreme cold delivers. During this epoch the spiritual life can either gain momentum as we search beneath the surface and plumb the spiritual depths, or become frozen tundra when we are overwhelmed by issues like declining health and personal hardships.

It is this winter season that we consider as we draw our reflections on hearing Abba's whisper to a close. Martin Marty reminds us that "winter is a season of the heart as much as it is a season in the weather," and he borrows from John Crowe Ransom the phrase "a cry of absence" to describe that connection.[1] The winter season of faith, in short, is characterized by the absence of God. The psalmist reminds us of God's constant presence, enjoining, "Where can I go from your spirit? Or where can I flee from your presence? If I ascend to heaven, you are there; if I make my bed in Sheol, you are there" (Ps 139:7–8). Theologically we embrace this tenet, but on an emotional level we often feel like God is indeed absent and a great chasm separates us from his arms of love. In any relationship there are times of withdrawal and absence. We are not continually with the ones we love. Due to my teaching in Bolivia I have been absent from my family each summer for ten years; it is part of the rhythm of our lives, bringing nurture in one area and absence in another.

At times we cry out to God for a greater experience of his presence and at other times God seeks us as the absent partner. The prophet Isaiah acknowledges God's waiting when he says, "I was ready to be sought out by those who did not ask, to be found by those who did not seek me. I said, "Here I am, here I am," to a nation that did not call on my name. I held out my hands all day long to a rebellious people, who walk in a way that is not good" (Isa 65:1–2). It is, as Isaiah points out, more likely that Abba calls out to us as the absent ones; our longing for him as the absentee Father is perhaps more feeble. Anthony Bloom insightfully adds that perhaps our felt distance from God's presence is an action of his mercy as we are often in no condition to be in his presence due to our lack of authenticity:

> To meet God face to face in prayer is a critical moment in our lives, and thanks be to Him that He does not always present Himself to us when we wish to meet Him, because we might not be able to endure such a meeting. . . . God is merciful. He does not come in an untimely way. He gives us a chance to judge ourselves, to understand, and not come into His presence at a moment when it would mean condemnation.[2]

Regardless, in the winter season we experience God's absence, and it is from that place that we look to one writer's experience in Psalm 137 to help us, so that our perception of silence does not become "a deadly silence" that enervates our trust in him.[3]

---

1. Marty, *Cry of Absence*, 1.
2. Bloom, *Beginning to Pray*, 27.
3. Doherty, *Poustinia*, 161.

Part II — The Practice of Listening

THERE WE HUNG OUR HARPS

There is a unique specificity to Psalm 137 as the psalmist locates his song "By the rivers of Babylon—there we sat down and there we wept when we remembered Zion" (v. 1). The exiled people have been relocated to Babylon after Jerusalem was razed in 587 BCE and are now away from their land and the temple of Yahweh. The people know that the holy land of Zion cannot simply be replaced by another piece of real estate, as their tormentors suggest—for the river plains of the Euphrates are not the same as the Judean hills. In dramatic fashion the musicians hang their harps on the nearby willows as a sign of protest when the oppressors seek performances of Zion's songs. They refuse to participate in this mockery of playing sacred songs as mere entertainment, crying out, "How could we sing the Lord's song in a foreign land?" (v. 4), and then invoke a curse on themselves: "If I forget you, O Jerusalem, let my right hand wither! Let my tongue cling to the roof of my mouth, if I do not remember you" (vv. 5–6). Surely this lament represents a firsthand experience of feeling the absence of God. They are "away" and a melancholic spirit pervades their cries as they long for home and for God's presence in a foreign land. At times we hear this melancholy in homesick students from Newfoundland who study at Tyndale in their expression, "We are away."

We see the coping mechanisms of the musicians represented in the psalm. The first response is to remember their experience in Jerusalem, shown in the words "when we remembered Zion" (v. 1). They find support as they reflect on their past service in the temple, worshiping and leading others in the praises of God—funding moments for the singers who now find themselves in exile. They reach back into the past to find a connecting point with God that buoys them up in the present. What are our funding moments that we can bring forward to sustain us in the present moment of absence? A time of baptism, confirmation, a personal epiphany, a special moment in creation, or a communal faith experience—all have the potential to sustain us in challenging times. The temptation is to dismiss such past experiences as irrelevant. But like the sad exiles in Babylon, we can allow these events—"when we remembered Zion"—to speak as true moments even though they seem distant. In my own life, I hold on to a cadre of past experiences from my youthful enthusiasm for God, which I continue to claim as part of my ongoing walk with Abba. These moments help to preserve me when I find myself in turbulent waters; they serve as touchstones, guiding me through the maze of confusion and self-doubt.

A second movement within the psalm is to not only remember God's faithfulness and action in the past, but to remember God in the present moment. The singer sings, "Let my tongue cling to the roof of my mouth, if I do not remember you" (v. 6)—that is, "if I do not remember you right now, even under the overcast of my new reality." What helps us to remember God during times of duress? One way is to recognize the help that can come from a sister or brother in the faith. Martin Marty uses the imagery of being carried by another:

> One can at least for part of the way "hitch-hike" on the spiritual experience of another . . . one can "barnacle" oneself to the word of another. One can be a "parasite" that lives off another spiritual organism. These words are not all lovely, not all positive sounding. But the hitchhiker does, or can, "get there."[4]

The singer can ride on the backs of the other singers or the elders with him in exile who have deeper roots in the faith. So we can grasp the hand of a trusted friend during our troublesome times. Who are our mentors? They can be individuals in the flesh or in the word—loving soul friends who encourage and support us, or writers from the past whose words resonate with our experience. The writings of Thomas Merton and Henri Nouwen have helped me immeasurably, a reminder that the church is made up of both the living and the dead. I have held on to their wisdom for twenty years through many ups and downs and have been sustained by their timely words. It is as if I hold up their photographs (which sometimes I even do!) and consider the lines and wrinkles on their faces, the joy in their eyes, and their smiles. These characteristics strengthen my resolve to go forward to finish the journey before me. The model of the psalmist to draw funding moments from the past and to hold on to others in the present allows me to receive strength to carry on in the sometimes dark and silent days of my present reality.

FALLOWNESS AS A HARBINGER OF HOPE

The psalm ends with shocking words:

> Remember, O Lord, against the Edomites the day of Jerusalem's fall, how they said, "Tear it down! Tear it down! Down to its foundations!" O daughter Babylon, you devastator! Happy shall they be

---

4. Marty, *Cry of Absence*, 27.

who pay you back what you have done to us! Happy shall they be
who take your little ones and dash them against the rock! (vv. 7–9)

It is a cry for the Lord's vengeance for the razing of Jerusalem and the destruction of its people—especially for the cruelty of destroying the innocents before their parents.[5] The psalmist identifies the alliance of the neighboring Edomites with the Babylonians in the destruction of Jerusalem and calls for the Lord's justice on their betrayal and on the violence of their captors. As upsetting as these vindictive statements are for present-day readers, they are ultimately an expression that seeks a future "remembering" of the Lord to bring about a balancing of the scales and a measure of justice. We surmise that on the other side of the anger the psalmist dreams of a future where peace is restored, the enemy is defeated, and the people once more dwell safely in the land of Zion. The psalmist's exclamations do not envision the reconciliation and prayers for the enemy that Jesus enjoins in the Sermon on the Mount (Matt 5:38–48), but they do look forward to a future rest from the enemy.

The challenge for the psalmist and for the nation of Israel is to perceive the absence from the land as a gift of fallowness, as the field's experience during the winter season. They have been separated from the land but are not rejected by the Lord. Yahweh will restore them to the land in the future; but their present work is to live creatively and honor God by continuing to rely on him even in the foreign land. In fact, the prophet Jeremiah instructs them not to remain depressed and incapacitated:

> Build houses and live in them; plant gardens and eat what they produce. Take wives and have sons and daughters; take wives for your sons, and give your daughters in marriage . . . seek the welfare of the city where I have sent you into exile, and pray to the Lord on its behalf, for in its welfare you will find your welfare. (Jer 29:6–7)[6]

It is a time of dormancy calling for active waiting and patient living before the God who is for them. It is not a time for forgetfulness but a time for vibrant listening for the quiet voice of the Father who never sleeps and constantly draws us with his subtle movements. We are not good at waiting or skilled in the art of patience. We want things immediately and find waiting stressful and frustrating. Perhaps our modern tendencies were known in the psalmist's day and the people also experienced waiting as a challenging

---

5. See Kidner, *Psalms 73–150*, 460.
6. See Jer 29:1–14.

venture. But at its best, the cry of the singer dreams a grander vision that finds a measure of equanimity in God's future shalom.

A modern-day parable of fallowness is found in the film *The Diving Bell and the Butterfly*. It tells the story of *Elle* magazine editor Jean-Dominique Bauby, who experiences a massive stroke at age forty-three, which leaves him with "locked-in syndrome"—a state in which he is fully aware but completely paralyzed except for the use of his left eye. He is devastated as he is transported from a life of prestige and success to being hospitalized and trapped in his body with seemingly no options for the future. Over time his family support and therapeutic team are able to draw him out of depression and he learns to communicate through a system connecting his eye movement with an alphabet board spelling out his words. Amazingly, he uses this time to slowly write a book, with the aid of others, revealing the fascinating journey of his interior world. His book *The Diving Bell and the Butterfly* contrasts his new "trapped" life in a diving bell with his imaginings of life as a butterfly. At one point of the book he writes:

> My diving bell becomes less oppressive, and my mind takes flight like a butterfly. There is so much to do. You can wander off in space or in time, set out for Tierra del Fuego or for King Midas's court. You can visit the woman you love, slide down beside her and stroke her still-sleeping face. You can build castles in Spain, steal the Golden Fleece, discover Atlantis, realize your childhood dreams and adult ambitions.[7]

The film portrays a person who receives a forced time of fallowness and is able to turn it into a fruitful experience of reclamation. Here the human spirit is able to overcome all odds and receive dormancy in a powerful and transformative manner. The author of the *The Diving Bell and the Butterfly* links with the passion of the psalmist who envisions a reality that is equally able to sustain a shocked community amidst the turbulence of the age.

THE CHALLENGE OF GOING FORWARD

The challenge is to experience the absence of God as fallowness and not as rejection. Abba is inviting us to wait upon him patiently and not become frustrated with the felt silence. How we respond in these times is our choice, each experience bringing its own psychological repercussions.

---

7. Bauby, *Diving Bell and the Butterfly*, 5.

Marty insightfully recognizes that we often turn away from God and feed in the shadows on our own peculiar compulsions. He illustrates this interior feeding frenzy by using the medieval terms "apathy, anomy, and acedia."[8] Apathy he describes as "being neither for nor against the abundance poured out on an already full life."[9] It is a state that evokes the response of not caring anymore about things material or spiritual. Life is perceived as too much work to add the exploration of "things unseen," so the springs of spiritual water dry up and the self-centered response of not "giving a damn" prevails. Following *apatheia* Marty identifies the little-known response of anomy, which he defines as "normlessness, an inability to care about standards when one is sated."[10] He describes it as "numb[ing] the sated heart, the one too long full of too many riches."[11] It speaks of the state of having much but being unmoved, evoking a spirit of ingratitude and malaise. Third, the ennui of acedia is added to the downward spiral, signifying the response of "restless boredom," or as Marty describes, "'leanness in the soul,' the wasting disease that comes to the fat and full."[12] This banal trinity is common among those who are well off and who expect the cheap grace that Bonhoeffer identified; they have little patience or energy to persist amidst the tropical depression that periodically sits over the soul.[13]

A parallel winter experience is described in another psalm, Psalm 37, where the poet describes the injustice of the ungodly succeeding in life's enterprises while the godly suffer and do not prosper. The righteous fret (vv. 3, 7, 8) and are both envious and angry over the prosperous and easy lifestyle of the wicked (vv. 1, 8), while the just are frequently forgotten and face constant challenges (vv. 14, 32, 35). The psalmist's thoughtful response is to keep waiting on God for the season of prosperity for the wicked is short (vv. 2, 9, 10) and the deeper longings of the soul are only satisfied in knowing God. The psalmist avers, "Take delight in the Lord, and he will give you the desires of your heart" (v. 4); "Wait for the Lord, and keep to his way, and he will exalt you to inherit the land" (v. 34); The wise teacher (v. 25) especially exhorts the listener, "Be still before the Lord, and wait patiently for him; do not fret over those who prosper in their way, over those who carry out

---

8. Marty, *Cry of Absence*, 156–57.
9. Ibid., 156.
10. Ibid.
11. Ibid., 157.
12. See Bondi, *To Love as God Loves*, 74; Marty, *Cry of Absence*, 157.
13. See Bonhoeffer, *Cost of Discipleship*, 45–46.

evil devices" (v. 7). The words to "be still" and "to wait" are active words, implying participation and demanding energy, not a passive twiddling of the thumbs until God acts. In fact, as one commentator suggests, "to be still and wait for God is not something which falls into the lap of man, but is the reward for the victory which man has gained in the struggle of his soul against his own assertive self."[14] We intentionally turn to him and silently wait in dependence for his revealed word.

It comes down to a question of focus. We can dwell on the injustices of life that fuel anger, frustration, and an apathetic spirit, but this perspective is rarely constructive; it simply isolates and diminishes our enthusiasm and passion for life. Or we can refocus on God, who is for us and provides the foundation for a meaningful and fruitful life in all our spheres of participation (vv. 39–40). We move in this direction by aligning our values with those expressed through God's love and seek to imitate his self-giving in our daily actions (Eph 5:1–2). It comes back to the reframing of absence as a season of fallowness in which space is provided to achieve its purposes of rest, recalibration, and rejuvenation.

ABSENCE IS NOT ABOUT FAILURE BUT ABOUT GROWTH

Absence is not about failure on our part but is a dimension of our relationship with God. We are relating to Abba as a person and all interpersonal dynamics have the tension of nearness and distance. Keating reminds us of this truth as he remembers the story of the royal official who asks Jesus to come to his house and heal his son. Instead, Jesus probes the official's faith by questioning his desire for a sign to initiate belief; he refuses to travel with him but tells him to return to his home for his son lives (John 4:46–54). The officer is left with a conundrum. Does he stay and argue his point or go in confidence believing Jesus' long-distance words are sufficient to effect healing? The father chooses the latter and his weak faith becomes stronger as he makes his journey home. His servants meet him on the road, joyfully announcing that his son lives; he realizes that the healing took place at the time of Jesus' words. In response to this exchange Keating comments on our own interior movements with Jesus: "The withdrawal of God's felt presence is meant to increase our faith, and without the withdrawal of that sensible presence we cannot but remain on this shallow level exemplified by the royal official." He goes on to say,

14. Weiser, *Psalms*, 318.

Part II — The Practice of Listening

> In our own spiritual growing up process we cannot escape the crisis of faith. This incident clearly teaches us that it is not merely a rebuke when Jesus seems to push us against the wall and to remove the props which we feel are so necessary for us. It is rather a call to new growth, to the transformation of our weakness. It is a call to a new union with him, a call to "launch out into the deep."[15]

Absence is a prompt to turn to God and say we want more, even as it challenges us not to settle but seek spiritual growth. God is constantly speaking to us at the most subtle levels, beckoning us to grow in our awareness of his presence. He uses the time of absence as a tool to draw us deeper so that we become more receptive to the Spirit's sensitive vibrations of love.

One of the ways of viewing this dance of intimacy and distance is to acknowledge that there is a rhythm to our lives, as we alluded to at the beginning of the chapter, that moves along with the image of the different seasons. The season of winter—which can strike us at different times—evokes a rhythm of silence or a stripping away to reveal what is most essential. In the diving world there is a lot of gear, including wetsuit, fins, mask, BCD, snorkel, computer; but what is most essential is the regulator and the air in the tank. Without air and a way to imbibe it one is lost. During a dive my daughter and I were forced to make a free one-hundred-foot ascent with a faulty regulator. We broke the surface on the last microsecond of breath. After recovering from the shock of the event, I was struck by the notion that the gear becomes completely useless without access to the air. Similarly, a spiritual stripping away reveals our need for dependence on the life-giving power of the Spirit of Jesus. Without his breath filling our lungs there is no life. Our faith diminishes into religiosity with no power or substance. It is like going to the beach and attempting to fly a great kite. Lift off seems impossible. We run and the kite drags behind us skimming the ground. Time and time again we try to fly it but to no avail. Suddenly, as if out of nowhere the kite lifts and races up into the sky, flying like a great rocket. The mystery of the wind is the essential ingredient that invigorates the entire process and it cannot be manipulated by our wishes. Likewise, the Holy Spirit remains the essential dimension of our faith journey and the stripping away process is periodically needed for us to be reminded of what is essential.

What rhythm are we walking to at this point in our journey? Is it the time of fullness or the time of barrenness? Is it the time of consolation or

---

15. Keating, *Crisis of Faith, Crisis of Love*, 22–23.

the time of desolation? In both God is speaking and we are invited to hear his voice. The writer of Ecclesiastes acknowledges the different rhythms of life in his poetic lines:

> For everything there is a season, and a time for every matter under heaven, a time to be born, and a time to die; a time to plant, and a time to pluck up what is planted; a time to kill, and a time to heal; a time to break down, and a time to build up; a time to weep, and a time to laugh; a time to mourn, and a time to dance. (3:1–4)

The time of silence, which he proceeds to identify (3:7), is the rhythm of minimalism and simplicity whereby one speaks and acts less so that vision and energy may increase. It is about waiting with outstretched, empty hands so they can be filled with heavenly gifts. Stripping away sounds jarring, painful, and uncomfortable, but it may be the action that is needed to revive waning embers so that the phoenix can rise and fly as the kite catching the wind on the strand. Saint John of the Cross identified these times as "the dark night of the soul," where one experiences loss, emptiness, and spiritual barrenness—all as a precursor for renewal.[16] The challenge we face is to recognize Abba's handiwork in calling us to new life amidst the darkness of the hour. When we are conscious of the spiritual rhythms that run in our veins at any given time, we more readily see God's purposes.

LISTENING AMIDST ABSENCE

The intentional action of remembering, as we noted in Psalm 137, includes remembering the times of intimacy with God, even during our times of absence. Recalling such moments has the power to stir our hearts in the here and now. There is a constant theme in Scripture to remain awake to the tiny vibrations of his love. The writers of the Psalms are frequently reminding us to be alert: "Morning by morning, O Lord, you hear my voice; morning by morning I lay my requests before you and wait in expectation" (5:3 NIV). "I believe that I shall see the goodness of the Lord in the land of the living. Wait for the Lord; be strong, and let your heart take courage; wait for the Lord!" (27:14). "Awake, my soul! Awake, O harp and lyre! I will awake the dawn. I will give thanks to you, O Lord, among the peoples; I will sing praises to you among the nations" (57:8–9). We have the opportunity to recognize the goodness of Abba in the rhythm of our day as we keep our spiritual eyes

---

16. St. John of the Cross, *Collected Works*, 355–56.

open. Consolation may not be our experience but we can still affirm his overtures as expressions of care and love. We have a friend suffering from cancer who has lost his wife through suicide—two shocking, life-changing blows. Quite remarkably he still demonstrates an ability to recognize God's hand through a song, an expression of care through a neighbor's action, a visit from a friend, serendipitous meetings on the street with old acquaintances, or a passage from a book. He carries many questions about his present experience but remains alert to the Spirit's movements amidst the storm. Remembering God's goodness (past and present) while being spiritually alert and waiting on his presence goes a long way to sustain us during the fallow times, even in dramatic seasons of pain such as his.

It is worth repeating that we travel better through the seasons of absence with the support of others. The touch of friends, family, and faith community bears us up while in the winter epoch. We have to be cognizant of our tendency to withdraw and cocoon ourselves during the times when we most need the presence of others. An example of such spiritual friendship is found in the life of Saint Anthony, the father of fourth-century monasticism. Anthony went into the desert to go deeper with God and at one point felt the call to live amongst the tombs in isolation to struggle with the forces of evil. This was a terrifying and demanding exercise but one he felt was essential for his own spiritual growth. Fortunately, during this time he was not completely alone; he had spiritual friends praying and bringing food to help him survive the physical and spiritual torment he was experiencing. Similarly, we benefit from having soul friends who are willing to walk with us through "the valley of death," bringing us solace while we bear the load of spiritual struggle and feel the absence of God.

We acknowledge that the timing and purposes of Abba amidst the seasons of absence do not necessarily mirror our own. A subsequent passage from the life of Anthony illustrates this point. While in the tombs the monk fell into a great battle with the devil and was racked with pain and tormented by demons in the shape of serpents and scorpions. The conflict was lengthy and Anthony suffered much duress but at the appointed time the Lord came to rescue him. After he was relieved from his torment Anthony asked the Lord why he tarried in coming to rescue him. To this query the Lord responded, "Anthony, I was right here, but I waited to see you in action. And now because you held out and did not surrender, I will always be your helper."[17]. Keating interprets the Lord's words with a challenge to us in our need for immediate comfort and relief:

> God holds back his infinite mercy from rushing to the rescue when we are in temptation and difficulties. He will not actively intervene because the struggle is opening and preparing every recess of our being for the divine energy of grace.... If the divine help comes too soon, before the work of purification and healing has been accomplished, it may frustrate our ultimate ability to live the divine life.[18]

The absence of Abba's consolation amidst the storms and during the winter season of faith enables us to spiritually find our feet and promotes the strengthening of our spiritual muscles.

Finally, there is the importance of maintaining one's spiritual routine during faith's winter season. At times it may strike us as little more than ritual due to the lack of experiential connection. But there is a place for such familiar practices when the foundations are shaking. Staying with our practice provides space for the Holy Spirit to make the little connections that are needed. If we cease our spiritual routine we remove the supports that help us to reconnect with God and undermine our greater desire for spiritual vitality. It is better to stay with our times of prayer, our communal gatherings, our reading of the Scriptures, our worship, and our celebration of the Eucharist. As we persevere and keep waiting on Abba the heavens eventually part, the human overcast subsides, and the clear skies of the balancing seasons speak and assuage our soul's thirst for the living God (Ps 42:1–2). If we are to hear the voice of God we must continue to look up, even if our glance is feeble and primarily the result of being carried by others. It is with this desire to see and hear that we ultimately receive the grace of hearing Abba's whisper.

---

17. Keating, *Foundations*, 195.
18. Ibid., 196.

Part II—The Practice of Listening

QUESTIONS FOR REFLECTION

1. In what ways have you experienced the winter season of God's absence?

2. Martin Marty identifies the three spiritual blocks of "apathy, anomy, and acedia" that do battle with our souls during the winter season. Have these or other forces challenged you in times of desolation? If so, how have you persevered through the storms of doubt and feeling the absence of God?

3. It is not uncommon to experience a sense of failure when God seems absent. But we have recognized that these times of absence can be God's way of drawing us to go deeper with him. Write in your journal about such a time and pause to remember how that experience drew you deeper into his love.

4. Spiritual friendship is key during the winter season of faith. There is a need to hitchhike on the back of a soul friend in such momentous times. Have you ever received or given this type of assistance to a friend in troubled waters? Share your experience with another as a means of encouragement.

Afterword

AS WE HAVE CONSIDERED the paths that lead us to Abba and the practices that connect us to his voice, we once again repeat the mantra "pay attention" to hear his subtle whispers. In her recent album *The Heart Speaks in Whispers*, the British R&B singer-songwriter Corrine Bailey Rae reminds us of the essential truth that we have to pay attention to hear the quiet murmurs that flow from our interior springs. "You've got to listen" to the whispers of the heart; otherwise they are lost or neglected in the commotion of life. It is this invitation to listen that we have been encouraging throughout the chapters of this book.

An example of this call to listen is found in the story of Nicodemus who comes to Jesus under the cover of night (John 3:1–21). He recognizes that Jesus must represent the teachings of God otherwise he could not perform the wondrous signs of healing and amazing demonstrations of power in his interactions with others on a daily basis. However, beyond this insight, Jesus baffles him because he does not fit into the religious paradigm that Nicodemus and the other Pharisees maintain. To break through the solidity of his prejudices Jesus shocks him by saying that to perceive spiritual matters one must "be born from above" (v. 3). Jesus adds ironically that as a respected teacher of Israel he should already know this truth! Nicodemus is puzzled by this call for rebirth and misses the point by interpreting the words literally, asking, "How can one re-enter the womb as an adult?" Jesus corrects him by clarifying that such a rebirth comes from the work of the Holy Spirit and speaks to an interior awakening that flows from the heart of God. Jesus embellishes his point with a metaphor: the mysterious work of God is subtle "like the wind blowing and we do not know the source of the wind" (v. 8). He is not speaking on a superficial, literal level (i.e., re-entering the birth canal) but is describing an internal dynamic that changes how we understand and connect with Abba. The process is not like a mathematical equation that we understand in an obvious four-step manner; rather we are invited to look within and listen closely for the new work that the Spirit is drawing forth from our subterranean depths. Jesus may well have added that many regular folk from his own neighborhood are hearing and understanding his message just fine, but the erudite teachers of the Law (like Nicodemus) are stuck in a rule-based tradition and unable to hear the creative loving overtures of Abba's voice.

The salient point from this interaction is Jesus' invitation to keep listening for Abba's life-giving whisper and not to become stuck in moribund structures. He is not going to hit us over the head with a proverbial two-by-four to get our attention but speaks through respectful quiet whispers that we must listen for and intentionally respond to. Merton says it is like listening to the distant ringing of bells—bells ringing and inviting one to life, like a carillon at a monastery calling the monks to drop their spades while working in the fields and gather for prayer in the monastic chapel. We must pay attention and listen for Abba's voice within the ebb and flow of daily life. Each day we are invited to open our eyes, ears, and hearts so that the Spirit's spontaneous combustion is released and received at our conscious and unconscious levels. If we keep hurrying from one event to another, living distracted lives, we miss the opportunities that constantly come our way. It is far more likely that the Father is speaking and we are not listening than the assumed corollary that we are listening and he is not speaking. The Father's love is like a mighty ocean, "deep, wide and high," and we are invited to experience it and indeed be "filled with all the fullness of God" (Eph 3:14–19). For this to take place we must be in tune with the Father of lights so that we receive his divine energy even as the earth receives the life-giving energy of the sun.

So as we draw to a close our reflections on listening for Abba's whispers, we conclude with a few simple suggestions. First, from the seven paths we have suggested, identify the prominent path that Abba employs to speak into your life. Throughout the coming week write down in your journal all of the times you hear his voice while walking this path. Nothing is too small to notice! Any time you are drawn by his voice make a note of it. Write it down so that you have something concrete to consider as you reflect on Abba's word for your life. Second, choose a subsequent path and sit with it for a week, writing in your journal about how Abba shows up in your life. Over a period of seven weeks cover all of the paths we have identified

Afterword

and observe the myriad of ways that Abba has whispered into your life. At the end of this first stage observe the connections between the different paths that Abba uses to address your life. For example, is there a connection between praising God and the sacramental dimensions that imprint the voice of Abba on your life? Or is there a connection between the paths of community and celebration whereby you experience the presence of God? As you make these connections (like drawing a mind map) you help to identify the mysterious communication web that Abba employs to nurture us in our relationship with the divine family.

Second, review the practices we have identified as we make our life journey. Using a similar approach, choose the first practice of paying attention and write down in your journal the specifics that speak to you of Abba. For example, we were walking along the coast at Neck Point, Nanaimo, and were suddenly greeted by a family of orcas just off shore! It was an amazing demonstration of Abba's creative power to see these massive creatures enjoying their own habitat while we appreciated their massive dorsal fins, stunning black and white bodies, and graceful fluidity. Nevertheless, one had to be paying attention to the undulating sea; otherwise the unexpected passing would be missed. The invitation is to truly look, see, and hear what is happening in your daily experience. As you do so, recognize the constant outpouring of Abba's gifts. As you go forward, add in the other practices to complement your listening apparatus. For example, link the dimension of time into the process of paying attention and then the aspect of land/space and observe how the synergy between the related practices speak and reveal the voice of God into your faith journey. We encourage you not to skip over any of the practices, as they all connect into the web of paths and practices that Abba uses to speak into our lives.

As we complete this process, we create a montage revealing the balanced, wise voice of Abba speaking into our lives. It is as if we are overhearing the "master designer"—the personification of wisdom spoken of in the Proverbs—engaging in his work and rejoicing in his relationship with the Source of Life:

> Then I was beside him, like a master worker;
> and I was daily his delight,
> rejoicing before him always,
> rejoicing in his inhabited world
> and delighting in the human race. (Prov 8:30–31)

Part II—The Practice of Listening

The wisdom teacher expands this image, revealing how Abba informs us and how we are able to tune in through ardent listening:

> And now, my children, *listen* to me:
> happy are those who keep my ways.
> *Hear* instruction and be wise,
> and do not neglect it.
> Happy is the one who *listens* to me,
> watching daily at my gates,
> *waiting* beside my doors.
> For whoever finds me finds life
> and obtains favour from the Lord . . .
> Come, eat of my bread
> and drink of the wine I have mixed.
> Lay aside immaturity, and *live*,
> and *walk in the way of insight*. (8:32-36; 9:5-6; italics added)

The ancient sage reminds us that God is not in the business of hiding himself. We do not live in the vacuum of deadly silence. Rather, Abba desires to make himself known and wants us to hear his voice and live in a dynamic relationship with the divine family. We are encouraged to press on, listening for his voice and walking in the paths that reveal his beauty and life. It is like walking an alpine trail through the meadows and around the glacier-fed lakes; we enjoy it best as we keep to the path so the that colorful display of the mountain flowers are fully appreciated and the panoramic vista admired. If we leave the path we may lose ourselves in the bog, forest, or fog, and see nothing of the mountain countryside. Better to stay on the trail, listening and fine-tuning the life-enhancing signals of Abba. As we do so the voice of the master designer is heard. Our place within his masterpiece becomes clear and our specific calling is revealed.

Bibliography

Abrams, M. H., and Stephen Greenblatt, eds. *The Norton Anthology of English Literature: The Major Authors.* 7th ed. New York: Norton, 2001.
Augustine. *Confessions.* Translated by R. S. Pine-Coffin. Harmondsworth, England: Penguin, 1961.
Austel, Hermann. "Shamah." In *TWOT* 938–39.
Avison, Margaret. *Always Now: The Collected Poems.* Vol. 2. Erin, ON: Porcupine's Quill, 2004.
———. *Momentary Dark.* Toronto: McClelland & Stewart, 2006.
Barclay, William. *Good Tidings of Great Joy.* Louisville: John Knox, 1999.
Barry, William. *Seek My Face.* Chicago: Loyola, 2009.
Bartholomew, Craig G., and Michael W. Goheen. *The Drama of Scripture: Finding Our Place in the Biblical Story.* Grand Rapids: Baker Academic, 2004.
Bauby, Jean-Dominique. *The Diving Bell and the Butterfly.* New York: Vintage, 1997.
Berry, Wendell. *What Are People For?* New York: North Point, 1990.
Blixen, Karen, and Gabriel Axel. *Babette's Feast.* Directed by Gabriel Axel, produced by Just Betzer. DVD. Denmark: Nordisk Films, 1987.
Bloom, Anthony. *Beginning to Pray.* New York: Paulist, 1970.
Bondi, Roberta. *To Pray and to Love: Conversations on Prayer with the Early Church.* Minneapolis: Fortress, 1991.
Bonhoeffer, Dietrich. *Life Together.* Translated by John W. Doberstein. New York: Harper & Row, 1954.
Brother Lawrence. *Practice of the Presence of God.* Translated by E. M. Blaiklock. Nashville: T. Nelson, 1981.
Brueggemann, Walter. *Finally Comes the Poet: Daring Speech for Proclamation.* Minneapolis: Fortress, 1989.
———. *The Message of the Psalms.* Minneapolis: Augsburg, 1984.
Bush, Russ, and Tom Nettles. *Baptists and the Bible.* Chicago: Moody, 1980.
Calvin, John. *Institutes of the Christian Religion.* Vol. 1. Edited by John McNeill. Philadelphia: Westminster, 1960.
Capon, Robert Farrar. *Kingdom, Grace, Judgment: Paradox, Outrage, and Vindication in the Parables of Jesus.* Grand Rapids: Eerdmans, 2002.
Chandor, J. C. *All Is Lost.* Directed by J. C. Chandor. Produced by Justin Nappi, et al. Lionsgate, 2013.
Craddock, Fred. *Philippians.* Interpretation. Atlanta: John Knox, 1985.

BIBLIOGRAPHY

Craven, Margaret. *The Owl Called My Name*. Toronto: Totem, 1975.
Dahood, Mitchell. *Psalms 51–100*. Anchor Bible 17. New York: Doubleday, 1968.
Davey, Alan, and Elizabeth Davey. *Climbing the Spiritual Mountain: The Questions of Jesus*. Eugene, OR: Wipf & Stock, 2014.
Dawn, Marva. *Keeping the Sabbath Wholly*. Grand Rapids: Eerdmans, 1989.
De Mello, Anthony. *One Minute Wisdom*. Garden City, NY: Doubleday, 1968.
De Waal, Esther. *Living with Contradiction: An Introduction to Benedictine Spirituality*. Harrisburg, PA: Morehouse, 1997.
———. *Seeking God: The Way of St. Benedict*. London: HarperCollins, 1996.
Dillard, Annie. *For the Time Being*. Toronto: Penguin, 1999.
———. *Pilgrim at Tinker Creek*. New York: Harper & Row, 1974.
———. *The Writing Life*. New York: HarperCollins, 1989.
Doherty, Catherine. *Poustinia*. Cobermere, ON: Madonna House, 2000.
Dorsey, Thomas. "Precious Lord, Take My Hand." Hill and Range Songs, 1938.
Earle, Ralph. *1, 2 Timothy*. Expositor's Bible Commentary 11. Grand Rapids: Zondervan, 1978.
English, Donald. *The Message of Mark*. Leicester: InterVarsity, 1992.
Farrell, Edward. *Beams of Prayer: Spiritual Reflections with Edward J. Farrell*. Edited by Lynn Salata. New York: Alba, 1999.
———. *The Father Is Very Fond of Me*. Denville, NJ: Dimension, 1975.
———. *Prayer Is a Hunger*. Denville, NJ: Dimension, 1972.
Freedman, David Noel, ed. *The Anchor Bible Dictionary*. 6 vols. New York: Doubleday, 1992.
Genova, Lisa, et al. *Still Alice*. Directed by Richard Glatzer and Wash Westmoreland, produced by James Brown et al. DVD. Sony Pictures Classics, 2014.
Green, Thomas. *Opening to God: A Guide to Prayer*. Notre Dame: Ave Maria, 1977.
Gunther, W. "Phileo." In *NIDNTT*, 2:547–79.
Guthrie, Donald. *The Pastoral Epistles*. Tyndale New Testament Commentaries. Grand Rapids: Eerdmans, 1976.
Hahn, H. C. "Chronos and Kairos." In *NIDNTT*, 3:839–45.
Hamilton, Rebecca. "Bridging Psychological Distance." *Harvard Business Review* 93 (March 2015) 116–19.
Hardy, Daniel, and David Ford. *Jubilate: Theology in Praise*. London: Darton, Longman and Todd, 1984.
Heschel, Abraham. *I Asked for Wonder: A Spiritual Anthology*. Edited by Samuel H. Dresner. New York: Crossroad, 1995.
———. *The Sabbath*. New York: Farrar, Straus and Giroux, 1976.
Houston, Jean. *Mystical Dogs: Animals as Guides to Our Inner Life*. San Francisco: New World Library, 2011.
Hughes, Richard T. *How Christian Faith Can Sustain the Life of the Mind*. Grand Rapids: Eerdmans, 2001.
Huxley, Laura. *This Timeless Moment*. New York: Farrar, Straus and Giroux, 1968.
Ivie, Brian. *The Drop Box*. Directed by Brian Ivie, produced by Will Tober and John Shepherd. DVD. Focus on the Family, 2014.
Janzen, W. "Land." In *The Anchor Bible Dictionary*, edited by David Noel Freedman, 4:143–54. New York: Doubleday, 1992.
John of the Cross. *The Collected Works of St. John of the Cross*. Translated by Kieran Kavanaugh and Otilio Rodriguez. Washington: ICS, 1991.

Bibliography

Jones, Spike. *Her*. Directed by Spike Jonze, produced by Megan Ellison and Vincent Landay. DVD. Warner Bros., 2013.
Keating, Thomas. *Crisis of Faith, Crisis of Love*. New York: Continuum, 1995.
———. *Foundations for Centering Prayer and the Christian Contemplative Life*. New York: Continuum, 2009.
———. *The Human Condition: Contemplation and Transformation*. New York: Paulist, 1999.
Kelly, J. N. D. *A Commentary on the Pastoral Epistles*. Grand Rapids: Baker, 1981.
Kelly, Thomas. *The Sanctuary of the Soul*. Nashville: Upper Room, 1997.
———. *A Testament of Devotion*. San Francisco: HarperSanFrancisco, 1992.
Kidner, Derek. *Psalms 1–72*. Downers Grove, IL: InterVarsity, 1975.
Kierkegaard, Søren. *Purity of Heart Is to Will One Thing: Spiritual Preparation for the Office of Confession*. Translated by Douglas V. Steere. New York: Harper & Row, 1956.
Knight, George Angus Fulton. *Psalms*. Vol. 1. Daily Study Bible. Philadelphia: Westminster, 1982.
Lamott, Anne. *Travelling Mercies: Some Thoughts on Faith*. New York: Random House, 1999.
Lewis, C. S. *A Grief Observed*. London: Faber & Faber, 1961.
———. *The Magician's Nephew*. New York: HarperCollins, 1983.
———. *The Problem of Pain*. New York: Macmillan, 1971.
———. *Reflections on the Psalms*. London: Collins, 1974.
———. *The Silver Chair*. New York: HarperCollins, 1981.
Lonergan, Bernard. *Insight: A Study of Human Understanding*. Toronto: University of Toronto Press, 2005.
———. *Method in Theology*. Toronto: University of Toronto Press, 2013.
Long, Thomas G. *Matthew*. Westminster Bible Companion. Louisville: Westminster John Knox, 1997.
May, Gerald. *Addiction and Grace: Love and Spirituality in the Healing of Addictions*. San Francisco: HarperSanFrancisco, 1988.
———. *The Awakened Heart: Opening Yourself to the Love You Need*. San Francisco: HarperCollins, 1991.
Mayer, Reinhold. "Feast" In *NIDNTT*, 2:624–32.
McNeill, Donald, et al. *Compassion: A Reflection on the Christian Life*. Garden City, NY: Doubleday, 1982.
Merton, Thomas. *Thoughts in Solitude*. Turnbridge Wells, UK: Burns & Oates, 1958.
Moore, Graham. *The Imitation Game*. Based on *Alan Turing: The Enigma* by Andrew Hodges. Directed by Morten Tyldum, produced by Nora Grossman et al. The Weinstein Co., 2014.
Muto, Susan, and Adrian van Kaam. *Practicing the Prayer of Presence*. Williston Park, NY: Resurrection, 1993.
Nachmanovitch, Stephen. *Free Play: Improvisation in Life and Art*. New York: Jeremy P. Tarcher/Putnam, 1990.
Nhat Hanh, Thich. *Living Buddah, Living Christ*. London: Rider, 1996.
Norris, Kathleen. *Acedia & Me: A Marriage, Monks, and a Writer's Life*. New York: Riverhead, 2008.
———. *Amazing Grace: A Vocabulary of Faith*. New York: Riverhead, 1998.
———. *The Cloister Walk*. New York: Berkley, 1997.
Nouwen, Henri. *Can You Drink the Cup?* Notre Dame: Ave Maria, 1996.
———. *A Cry for Mercy*. Garden City, NY: Image, 1983.

Bibliography

———. *Reaching Out: The Three Movements of the Spiritual Life.* New York: Doubleday, 1975.

———. *The Road to Daybreak: A Spiritual Journey.* New York: Doubleday, 1988

———. *Spiritual Direction: Wisdom for the Long Walk of Faith.* With Michael Christensen and Rebecca Laird. New York: HarperCollins, 2006.

———. *With Open Hands.* New York: Ballantine, 1985.

Nouwen, Henri, and Walter Gaffney. *Aging: The Fulfillment of Life.* New York: Doubleday, 1976.

Orr, James. "Immortality in the Old Testament." In *Classical Evangelical Essays in Old Testament Interpretation,* edited by Walter C. Kaiser Jr., 253–65. Grand Rapids: Baker, 1972.

Palmer, Earl. *Integrity: A Commentary on the Book of Philippians.* Vancouver: Regent College Publishing, 1992.

Peck, M. Scott. *The Different Drum: Community Making and Peace.* New York: Simon & Schuster, 1987.

Pemberton, Cintra. *Soulfaring: Celtic Pilgrimage Then and Now.* London: SPCK, 1999.

Peterson, Eugene. *A Long Obedience in the Same Direction.* Downers Grove, IL: InterVarsity, 1980.

Postema, Don. *Space for God: Study and Practice of Spirituality and Prayer.* 2nd ed. Grand Rapids: CRC, 1997.

Rahner, Karl. *The Practice of Faith.* New York: Crossroad, 1992.

Roderick, Philip, and Henri Nouwen. *Beloved: Henri Nouwen in Conversation.* Toronto: Novalis, 2007.

Rolheiser, Ronald. *Forgotten Among the Lilies: Learning to Love Beyond Our Fears.* New York: Galilee/Doubleday, 2005.

Schattenmann, J. "Koinonia." In *NIDNTT,* 1:639–44.

Smedes, Lewis. *How Can It Be All Right When Everything Is All Wrong?* San Franciso: HarperSanFranciso, 1992.

Smith, C. Christopher, and John Pattison. *Slow Church: Cultivating Community in the Patient Way of Jesus.* Downers Grove, IL: InterVarsity, 2014.

Steindl-Rast, David. *Gratefulness, the Heart of Prayer: An Approach to Life in Fullness.* New York: Paulist, 1984.

Strassfeld, Michael. *The Jewish Holidays: A Guide and Commentary.* New York: Harper & Row, 1985.

Teilhard de Chardin. *The Divine Milieu.* New York: Harper & Row, 1960.

Teresa of Avila *The Interior Castle.* Translated and edited by E. Allison Peers. New York: Doubleday, 1961.

Tolle, Eckhart. *The Power of Now.* Novato, CA: New World Library, 1999.

Tracey, Brian. "Seven Steps to Developing a New Habit." http://www.briantracy.com/blog/personal-success/seven-steps-to-developing-a-new-habit/.

Underhill, Evelyn. *Concerning the Inner Life.* Oxford: Oneworld, 1995.

———. *The Spiritual Life.* London: Hodder & Stoughton, 1996.

———. *Worship.* New York: Crossroad, 1982.

Van Breemen, Peter G. *Let All God's Glory Through.* New York: Paulist, 1993.

———. *The God Who Won't Let Go.* Notre Dame: Ave Maria, 2001.

Vanier, Jean. *Becoming Human.* Toronto: House of Anansi, 1998.

———. *The Broken Body: Journey to Wholeness.* London: Darton, Longman and Todd, 1999.

Bibliography

———. *Community and Growth*. London: Darton, Longman and Todd, 1990.
———. *Drawn into the Mystery of Jesus*. Toronto: Novalis, 2004.
———. "The Mystery of Being and Growth." *Images of Love, Words of Hope: Jean Vanier in Conversation*. Toronto: Norflicks Productions, 1988.
———. "Seeing God in Others." https://www.youtube.com/watch?v=k_xDRTXb-_o.
Visser, Margaret. *Beyond Fate*. Toronto: House of Anansi, 2002.
Webb, Paul, and Ava DuVernay. *Selma*. Directed by Ava DuVernay, produced by Oprah Winfrey, et al. DVD. Paramount, 2014.
Webber, Robert E. *Worship Is a Verb*. Waco, TX: Word, 1985.
Weiser, Arthur. *The Psalms*. Philadelphia: Westminster, 1962.
Westermann, Claus. *Praise and Lament in the Psalms*. Atlanta: John Knox, 1981.
Willard, Dallas. *The Divine Conspiracy*. New York: HarperCollins, 1998.
Willimon, William H. *Acts*. Interpretation. Atlanta: John Knox, 1988.
———. *The Bible: A Sustaining Presence in Worship*. Valley Forge, PA: Judson, 1981.
Wright, N. T. *Paul for Everyone: The Prison Letters: Ephesians, Philippians, Colossians, and Philemon*. London: SPCK, 2002.
Yaconelli, Mike. *Messy Spirituality: Christianity for the Rest of Us*. London: Hodder & Stoughton, 2001.

www.ingramcontent.com/pod-product-compliance
Lightning Source LLC
Chambersburg PA
CBHW050803160426
43192CB00010B/1618